THEA

A Theatre503 production

WOLFIE

some sort of fairytale

BY ROSS WILLIS

Wolfie was a 503Five seed commission with Theatre503, and was first performed at Theatre503, London, on 20 March 2019.

WOLFIE

some sort of fairytale

BY ROSS WILLIS

CAST

Z   Erin Doherty
A   Sophie Melville

CREATIVE TEAM

Director	Lisa Spirling
Designer	Basia Bińkowska
Lighting Designer	Rajiv Pattani
Sound Designer and Composer	Richard Hammarton
Movement Director	Belinda Lee Chapman
Casting Director	Annelie Powell CDG
Assistant Director	Sara Aniqah Malik
Creative Trainee	Paige Crimp

PRODUCTION TEAM

Producer	Jake Orr
Production Manager	Callum Finn
Stage Manager	Rose Hockaday
Scenic Artist	Steven Peters
PR	Nancy Poole
Assistant Producers	Adam Line and Jessica Moncur

CAST

ERIN DOHERTY – Z
Erin trained at Bristol Old Vic Theatre School.

Theatre credits include: *The Divide* (Old Vic and Edinburgh International Festival); *A Christmas Carol* (Old Vic); *My Name is Rachel Corrie* (Young Vic); *Junkyard* (Headlong/Bristol Old Vic/Theatr Clywd/Rose Kingston); *Wish List* (Manchester Royal Exchange and Royal Court; Winner: Best Actress, Manchester Theatre Award); *Who Cares* (The Lowry); *The Glass Menagerie* (tour); *Pink Mist* (Bristol Old Vic).

Television credits include: *Call the Midwife*, *Les Misérables* (BBC).

Forthcoming television includes: Princess Anne in *The Crown* (Netflix).

Erin is an Evening Standard Rising Star 2018 and a Screen International Star of Tomorrow 2018. She was also the recipient of The Stephen Sondheim Society Student Performer of the Year 2015.

SOPHIE MELVILLE – A
Sophie trained at Royal Welsh College of Music and Drama.

Theatre credits include: *Blue* (Chapter Theatre); *Close Quarters* (Sheffield Crucible); *Pops* (Young Vic); *No One Will Tell Me How to Start a Revolution* (Hampstead); *The Divide* and *Pagans* (Old Vic); *Low Level Panic* (Orange Tree); *2066* (Almeida); *Blackbird* (The Other Room Theatre; Winner: Best Female Performance, Wales Theatre Awards); *Insignificance* (Theatr Clwyd); *Iphigenia in Splott* (National Theatre/Theater 59E59 NYC, The Sherman, Edinburgh Fringe Festival and international tour; Winner: The Stage Award for Acting Excellence, and Best Female Performance, Wales Theatre Award. Evening Standard Award nomination for Best Actress, Drama Desk Award nomination for Outstanding Solo Performance); *Romeo and Juliet* (Sherman); *Under Milk Wood* (Theatr Clwyd Cymru); *The Shape of Things*; *'Tis a Pity She's a Whore*; *See How They Run* (Theatre by the Lake); *Romeo and Juliet* (The Sam Wanamaker Festival).

Television credits include: *The Left Behind*, *The Missing 2* (BBC).

CREATIVE TEAM

ROSS WILLIS – WRITER

Ross is currently one of Theatre503's resident playwrights, the 503Five, where he received a commission to write *Wolfie*. He is a member of the Orange Tree Writers' Collective, BBC Writersroom and a playwright on attachment at the Bristol Old Vic. He was the Writer in Residence at Theatr Clwyd, an alumnus of Tamasha Playwrights '16/'17 and Soho Theatre Writers' Lab, where he developed *Wonder Boy*, which was a Tony Craze Award finalist and was produced by Bristol Old Vic Theatre School. He was commissioned by Tamasha and Titilola Dawudu to write four monologues for *Hear Me Now*, a book of monologues for diverse actors, and collaborated with Arcola Youth Theatre on the play *We Make Fire*. He is currently under commission to LAMDA and Audible, and has recently been announced as one of three writers awarded the inaugural Royal Court and Kudos Writing Fellowship.

LISA SPIRLING – DIRECTOR

Lisa Spirling is the Artistic Director of Theatre503. Previously she was the coordinator of the JMK Trust Regional Director's Program and a founder of Buckle for Dust Theatre Company.

Productions include: *Describe the Night* (Hampstead); *In Event of Moone Disaster* (Theatre503); *Jumpy* (Theatr Clwyd), *Ken, Deposit, Fault Lines* and *I Know How I Feel About Eve* (Hampstead); *Hello / Goodbye* (Singapore Rep Theatre); *The Nine O'Clock Slot* (Ice & Fire Theatre Company/Red Gallery); *Donkeys' Years* and *Here* (Rose, Kingston); *Hundreds & Thousands* (Buckle for Dust/English Touring Theatre Soho); *Cotton Wool* (Buckle for Dust/Theatre503); *Boeing Boeing* (Alley Theatre, Texas); *The Vagina Monologues* and *Gas and Air* (Pleasance, London).

BASIA BIŃKOWSKA – DESIGNER

Basia is a BA Theatre Design graduate from the Royal Conservatoire of Scotland. After her graduation she completed the Trainee Designer Scheme at the Royal Shakespeare Company. She is the Overall Winner of the Linbury Prize for Stage Design 2017, and also Best Designer Nominee for The Stage Debut Awards 2018.

Basia's credits include: *othellomacbeth* (Lyric Hammersmith/HOME Manchester); *Cuckoo* (Soho); *5 plays* (Young Vic); *Devil with a Blue Dress* (Bunker); *Reactor* (ArtsEd London); *Working* (Royal Academy of Music); *Sweet Smell of Success* (Royal Academy of Music).

Her upcoming work includes: *Blood Knot* (Orange Tree); *Acts of Resistance* (Headlong/Bristol Old Vic); *Crooked Dances* (Royal Shakespeare Company) and *Ivan and the Dogs* (Young Vic).

RAJIV PATTANI – LIGHTING DESIGNER

Rajiv graduated from LAMDA in 2014 with qualifications in Stage Management and Technical Theatre, specialising in Lighting & AV.

Theatre includes: *Babylon Beyond Borders* (Bush/live-streamed to NYC, São Paulo, Johannesburg); *Leave Taking, Dismantle This Room, Hijabi Monologues London* (Bush); *Ramona Tells Jim* (Bush Studio); *Bullet Hole* (Park); *Roman Candle* (Theatre503/Manchester 53Two/Edinburgh Fringe Festival); *NASSIM* (Traverse, Edinburgh/Bush/

international tour; Winner: Edinburgh Fringe First); Bush Theatre's reopening event *Black Lives, Black Words*; *STUD* (Network Theatre, VAULT Festival); *Screaming Secrets & Glass Roots* (Tristan Bates).

Freelance lighting design includes: *On the Razzle* and *Rabbit* (Pleasance) *Blood Wedding* (Bread and Roses); *Might Never Happen* (Doll's Eye Theatre Company); *Primadonna* (VAULT Festival); as well as various projects at the Arcola, Hampstead and the Unicorn.

Rajiv was also Production Electrician on *Four minutes twelve seconds* (Trafalgar Studios).

RICHARD HAMMARTON – SOUND DESIGNER AND COMPOSER
Theatre credits include: *Princess & The Hustler* (Eclipse Theatre Company); *Lost Paradise* (New Visual Paradigm); *Under Milk Wood* (Northern Stage); *Women in Power* (Nuffield); *Describe the Night, Deposit, Sunspots* (Hampstead); *Out Of Sight* (fanShen tour); *Jekyll and Hyde* (Touring Consortium Theatre Company); *Love from a Stranger, Someone Who'll Watch Over Me* (Royal & Derngate, Northampton); *Hanna, Trestle, Orca, Tomcat* (Papatango); *In Event of Moone Disaster* (Theatre503); *Burning Doors* (Belarus Free Theatre); *Girls* (HighTide); *The Weir* (English Touring Theatre); *As You Like It, An Inspector Calls* (Theatre by the Lake); *Traitor* (Pilot); *Faust x2* (Watermill); *Dirty Great Love Story* (Arts); *Assata Taught Me* (Gate); *Low Level Panic* (Orange Tree); *Luv* (Park); *Much Ado About Nothing, Jumpy* (Theatr Clwyd); *Linda* (Royal Court); *The Crucible* (Manchester Royal Exchange); *Comrade Fiasco* (Gate); *A Number* (Nuffield/Young Vic); *Beached* (Marlowe Theatre/Soho); *Grimm Tales 2* (Bargehouse, Oxo Tower Wharf); *Ghost from a Perfect Place* (Arcola); *The Crucible* (Old Vic); *Dealer's Choice* (Royal & Derngate, Northampton); *Sizwe Bansi is Dead* (Theatre Royal Stratford East/UK tour); *Kingston 14* (Theatre Royal Stratford East); *Brilliant Adventures, Dr Faustus* (Winner of MEN Best Design Award), *Edward II* (Manchester Royal Exchange); *Bandages* (TEG Productions); *The Last Summer* (Gate, Dublin); *The Pitchfork Disney* (Arcola); *Six Characters Looking for an Author* (Young Vic); *Mudlarks* (Hightide Festival/Theatre503/Bush).

Television credits include: *Ripper Street, No Win No Fee, Sex 'n' Death, Wipeout, The Ship* (BBC); *Agatha Christie's Marple* (ITV);

Radio credits include: *The Effect* (BBC Radio 3).

Orchestration work: *Agatha Christie's Marple* series 1 & 2, *Primeval, Jericho, If I Had You* (ITV); *Dracula, A History of Britain, Silent Witness, Dalziel and Pascoe* (BBC); *Alice Through the Looking Glass* (Channel 4); *The Nine Lives of Tomas Katz* and *Scenes of a Sexual Nature* (feature films, UK).

BELINDA LEE CHAPMAN – MOVEMENT DIRECTOR
Belinda trained at English National Ballet School, London School of Puppetry and Philippe Gaulier, Paris. She performed and devised leading roles for Matthew Bourne's New Adventures productions and is a fellow of The Arts Foundation as Creator of Theatre for Young People. She founded B2B Theatre that was resident at The Corn Exchange Newbury.

Belinda's movement direction and choreography credits include: *My Shout* (New Adventures); *Macbeth* (National Youth Theatre); *Girl with the Iron Claws* (The Wrong Crowd); *Monkey!* (UK tour); *London School of Puppetry* (Poet Lavel, France Festival); *War Torn* (Theatre Royal Plymouth); *The Night Time Whisperers* (Corn Exchange

Newbury); *The Odd Stock Curse* (Sailsbury Arts Centre); *The Maids* (Battersea Arts Centre); *Pandora's Box* (Company of Angels, Drama Centre); the role of Shiela in *Play Without Words* (New Adventures, National Theatre); *The Hunt* (BAFTA cinema) and *Together* (English National Ballet School).

Performance and theatre credits include: *Swamped* (Hall For Cornwall); *The Lise Meitner story* (QE Science); *We'll Meet in Moscow* (Phoenix); *The Odd Stock Curse* (Sailsbury Arts Centre); *Hotel Follies* (Arts, West End); *Unfolding Layers* (The Place, London); *The Maids* (Battersea Arts Centre); *La Belle Helen* (Royal Opera House); *Mahabharata* (Sadler's Wells); *Play Without Words* (National Theatre/Bunkamura Japan); *Ruby and the Big Top* (UK tour); *Masquerade* (Royal Opera House); *The Sandwich* (Tristan Bates); *The Nutcracker!* (Sadler's Wells/UK tour); *The Car Man* (Old Vic/Bunkamura Japan/Ahmanson LA); *Faust* (English National Opera) *Swan Lake* (Dominion Theatre/UK tour); *Cinderella* (Ahmanson Theatre LA); *Parsifal* (English National Opera); *Voyeurz* (Whitehall Theatre)

Film and TV includes: *Hippy Shake*, Complicité Theatre (OZ Films); *Never Say Die* (BBC); *Nutcracker! New Adventures, London Transport Doc* and *Class Act* (ITV)

ANNELIE POWELL CDG – CASTING DIRECTOR
Following five years casting at the Royal Shakespeare Company, Annelie was appointed Head of Casting at the Nuffield Southampton Theatres in 2017. Her recent work there includes: John Brittain's Musical of David Walliams' *Billionaire Boy* (dir. Luke Sheppard); Howard Brenton's *The Shadow Factory* (dir. Sam Hodges); *A Streetcar Named Desire* (dir. Chelsea Walker, also for Theatr Clwyd & English Touring Theatre), and *Fantastic Mr. Fox* (dir. by Maria Aberg).

Annelie continues to work prolifically as a freelance casting director. Upcoming and recent projects include: *Vassa* (Almeida); *Cougar* (Orange Tree); *Don Carlos* starring Tom Burke (UK tour); Angus Jackson's *Don Quixote* (Royal Shakespeare Company/West End); Richard Twyman's version of *Othello* (English Touring Theatre), *Describe the Night* (Hampstead), *othellomacbeth* (Lyric Hammersmith/HOME) and *In Event of Moone Disaster* (Theatre503).

Select credits for the Royal Shakespeare Company include: *Hamlet* (dir. Simon Godwin), *King Lear*, *Imperium* (dir. Gregory Doran); *The Rover* (dir. Loveday Ingram); *Seven Acts of Mercy* (dir. Erica Whyman); *Two Noble Kinsman* (dir. Blanche McIntyre); *Wendy and Peter Pan* (dir. Jonathan Munby); *Oppenheimer* (dir. Angus Jackson, inc. West End transfer), and *The Shoemaker's Holiday* (dir. Philip Breen).

SARA ANIQAH MALIK – ASSISTANT DIRECTOR
Sara is currently training as a Director at Bristol Old Vic Theatre School.

As Director her credits include: *Salaam* (VAULT Festival), *A Streetcar Named Desire*, *The Tempest*, *The Crucible* (King's College London).

As Assistant Director her credits include: *Mrs Beeton Says: The Musical* (Redgrave Theatre), *The Comedy of Errors* (Edinburgh Fringe Festival), *Clybourne Park* (Tower Theatre), *The Breaks in You & I* (Hope Theatre).

PAIGE CRIMP – CREATIVE TRAINEE
Paige joined the creative team of *Wolfie* as a Creative Trainee after leaving school and deciding that theatre is one of her greatest passions and that she would like a career in it. This is her first proper behind-the-scenes theatre role and she is super-excited to be working on this fantastic and highly anticipated production at Theatre503.

PRODUCTION TEAM

JAKE ORR – PRODUCER

Jake is Producer for Theatre503. Before joining Theatre503, Jake was a freelance producer and programmer. In 2009 he founded A Younger Theatre, an organisation that supports and nurtures young people through journalism training. In 2014 Jake co-founded Incoming Festival with New Diorama Theatre, a festival that supports emerging theatre companies. Jake is also co-director of producing company Making Room and Director of Jake Orr Productions.

Jake's producing credits include; *Cinderella and the Beanstalk* (Theatre503); *Br'er Cotton* (Theatre503; Winner: Best New Play Off West End Awards); *In Event of Moone Disaster* (Theatre503; Winner: Best New Writer Stage Debut Awards); *No Miracles Here* (The Letter Room at Edinburgh Festival Fringe/Northern Stage/The Lowry/Shoreditch Town Hall); *BLUSH* (Snuff Box Theatre at Edinburgh Fringe Festival/Soho/Tour; Winner: The Stage Award); *Weald* (Snuff Box Theatre/Finborough) and *Shelter Me* (Circumference/Theatre Delicatessen).

As co-producer his credits include *The Art of Gaman* (Theatre503); *Gutted* (HOME, Manchester/Edinburgh Festival Fringe); *COW* (Edinburgh Festival Fringe) and *Sticking* (national tour).

As Associate Producer his credits include *Lists for the End of the World* (Edinburgh Festival Fringe); *The Bombing of the Grand Hotel* (Cockpit/tour), *Mouse Plague* (Edinburgh Festival Fringe/BAC/tour) and *The Eradication of Schizophrenia in Western Lapland* (Edinburgh Festival Fringe/BAC/tour).

Jake was nominated for Best Producer in the 2014 Off West End Awards.

CALLUM FINN – PRODUCTION MANAGER

Callum is a freelance Production Manager who holds a BA (Hons) in Production and Stage Management from the Royal Academy of Dramatic Art.

Recent theatre credits include: *All is True* (Southwark Playhouse); *Pinocchio* (Immersion Theatr/UK tour); *Grandad's Island* (Engine House Theatre, UK/Geneva tour); *A Crag Path Christmas* (AJH); *Cinderella and the Beanstalk* (Theatre503); *Seussical* (Southwark Playhouse); *Drowned or Saved?* (Tristan Bates); *Euroboat* (Viking Line Cruises); *Daisy Pulls It Off* (Park); *Hamlet* (KBTC).

Film credits include: *Artemis Fowl* (Disney) and *All is True* (TKBC).

Previously Callum worked as Assistant Head of Production at RADA.

ROSE HOCKADAY – STAGE MANAGER

Rose Hockaday graduated from Rose Bruford in 2014 with a degree in Lighting Design, and has since been working as a Freelance Lighting Technician & Stage Manager in London.

Theatre: *The Ex-Boyfriend Yard Sale* (Camden People's Theatre); *Art of Gaman* (Theatre503); *You Only Live Forever* and *In Tents and Purposes* (Viscera Theatre); *Timmy, Glitter Punch, Sophie, Ben and Other Problems, The Festival of Spanish Theatre, How to Survive a Post-Truth Apocalypse, They Built It. No One Came* and *Jericho Creek* (Fledgling Theatre); *A View from Islington North* (Out of Joint) and *The Angry Brigade* (Paines Plough).

Film: *Heaven Knows, Visitors, Ignite, Pomegranate, Wandering Eyes,* and *Versions of Us.* As well as music videos *Phase Me Out, When You're Gone,* and *Saint* for artist VÉRITÉ.

ADAM LINE – ASSISTANT PRODUCER
Adam is a Freelance Producer, currently a Resident Assistant Producer at Theatre503.
Recent credits include *CAUSE* (VAULT Festival, Producer); *The Inevitable Disappearance
of Edward J. Neverwhere* (BasicSpace Festival, Co-Producer); *Valiant* (Women in War
Festival, Associate Producer), *Measure for Measure* (Rose Playhouse, Production
Assistant).

JESSICA MONCUR – ASSISTANT PRODUCER
Jess is currently a Resident Assistant Producer at Theatre503. Producing credits
include: *Jerusalem* and *Assassins* (Stage@Leeds). Other creative credits include *Liz,
Forgive Us, Oh Father!* (Edinburgh Festival Fringe) and *Rules for Living* (Stage@Leeds).
Jess is also the incoming Producer for Blueleaf Theatre.

THEATRE 503

Theatre503 is the home of new writers and a launchpad for the artists who bring their words to life. We are pioneers in supporting new writers and a champion of their role in the theatre ecology. We find exceptional playwrights who will define the canon for the next generation. Learning and career development are at the core of what we do. We stage the work of more debut and emerging writers than any other theatre in the country. In the last year alone we staged 60 productions featuring 133 writers from short plays to full runs of superb drama and launching over 1,000 artists in the process. We passionately believe the most important element in a writer's development is to see their work developed through to a full production on stage, performed to the highest professional standard in front of an audience.

Over the last decade, many first-time writers have gone on to establish a career in the industry thanks to the support of Theatre503: Tom Morton-Smith (*Oppenheimer*, RSC and West End), Anna Jordan (Bruntwood Prize Winner for *Yen*, Royal Exchange, Royal Court and Broadway), Vinay Patel (writer of the BAFTA winning *Murdered By My Father*), Katori Hall (*Mountaintop*, 503, West End & Broadway – winner of 503's first Olivier Award) and Jon Brittain (*Rotterdam* – winner of our second Olivier Award in 2017).

Theatre503 Team

Artistic Director	Lisa Spirling
Executive Director	Andrew Shepherd
Producer	Jake Orr
Literary Manager	Steve Harper
General Manager	Anna De Freitas
Marketing Coordinator	Jennifer Oliver
Technical Manager	Alastair Borland
Literary Associate	Lauretta Barrow
Operations Assistant	Nyanna Bentham-Prince
Resident Assistant Producers	Natalie Chan, Adam Line, Jessica Moncur
Intern	Katarina Grabowsky

Theatre503 Board

Erica Whyman OBE (Chair)
Royce Bell (Vice Chair)
Chris Campbell
Joachim Fleury
Celine Gagnon
Eleanor Lloyd
Marcus Markou
Geraldine Sharpe-Newton
Jack Tilbury
Roy Williams OBE

Theatre503 Volunteers

Kelly Agredo, Emma Anderson, Elisabth Barbay, Hannah Bates, Emily Brearley-Bayliss, Alex Brent, Théo Buvat, Harley Cameron-Furze, Georgia Cusworth, Debra Dempster, Imogen Dobie, Uju Enendu, Rachel Gemaehling, Ashley Jones, Gareth Jones, Sian Legg, Andri Leonido, George Linfield, Ceri Lothian, Graham McCulloch, Ellen McGahey, Georgia McKnight, Tom Mellors, Annabel Pemberton, Lucy Robso, Kate Roche, Hannah Sands, Sussan Sanii, Kamilah Shorey, Ellie Snow, Paul Sockett, Caroline Summers Ayaaz Tariq, Thanos Topouzis, Melisa Tehrani, Camilla Walters, Stephanie Withers.

503Five

Ross Willis was part of Theatre503's 503Five, a pioneering 18-month writers' residency, where five exceptional writers on the cusp of a full production are given a seed commission to write and develop a feature-length play, as well as mentoring, workshops and dramaturgical support. We commit to staging at least one script and, where possible, try and work with other companies to develop the other scripts either at 503 or in another home. We could not do this without the incredible support of the Carne Trust who cover the costs of the seed commission and so far have helped 20 writers. We are also thrilled to welcome The Orseis Trust who have not only supported Ross to develop his script beyond his submitted draft to the production, but also enabled 503 to support Yasmin Joseph's script of *J'Ouvert* in the same season.

The 503Five alumni are Brad Birch, Jon Brittain, Ella Greenhill, Charlene James, Gemma Langford, Christopher Hogg, Yasmin Joseph, Richard Marsh, Brian Mullin, Rex Obano, Neasa O'Callaghan, Lou Ramsden, Nimer Rashed, Beth Steel, Chloe Todd Fordham, Chris Urch, Ross Willis, Aisha Zia. Between them they have been commissioned, nominated for and won countless awards including a BAFTA, The Bruntwood Prize, The Evening Standard Charles Wintour Award for Most Promising Playwright and an Olivier Award.

OUR SUPPORTERS

We are particularly grateful to Philip and Christine Carne and the long term support of The Carne Trust for our Playwriting Award and 503Five.

Share The Drama Patrons: Angela Hyde-Courtney, Eilene Davidson, Cas & Philip Donald, David Baxter, Erica Whyman, Geraldine Sharpe-Newton, James Bell, Jill Segal, Joakim Fleury, Nick Hern, Marcus Markou, Mike Morfey, Pam Alexander, Patricia Hamzahee, Robert O'Dowd, Roger Booker, Richard Bean, Rotha Bell, Sean Winnett.

Theatre Refurbishment: Jack Tilbury, Plann, Dynamis, CharcoalBlue, Stage Solutions, Will Bowen, The Theatres Trust.

The Foyle Foundation, Arts Council England National Lottery Projects Grant, The Peter Wolff Foundation (503 Production Fund), The Orseis Trust (503Five), Battersea Power Station Foundation (Right to Write) Barbara Broccoli/EON, Wimbledon Community Foundation (Five-O-Fresh), Nick Hern Books (503 Playwriting Award), Wandsworth Borough Council.

Theatre503 is in receipt of funding from Arts Council England's Catalyst: Evolve fund, match funding every pound raised in new income until July 2019.

SPECIAL THANKS

Theatre503 would like to thank the following people for their support on Wolfie: Isabelle Culkin, Rhys Newcombe-Jones, Katarina Grabowsky, Nichole Bird, Danielle Bird, Marcus Markou, Emma Banwell and Lizzie Props LTD, the second year students at ALRA, Betsy Blatchley, The Diocese of Southwark and the Bush Theatre.

Hugs and High-Fives to

Lisa Spirling, Steve Harper, Andrew Shepherd, Jake Orr, Katarina Grabowsky, Anna DeFreitas, Lauretta Barrow, Jennifer Oliver, Adam Line, Jessica Moncur and everyone at Theatre503.

My early readers Fin Kennedy, Rabiah Hussain, Matilda Ibini, Yasmeen Khan, Guleraana Mir Afshan D'souza-Lodhi, Ayesha Siddiqi and Dianna Hunt (Tamafia), Yasmin Joseph, Mahad Ali, Chris Hogg and Aisha Zia.

Nadia Latif, Tom Powell, Lucy Morrison, Dennis Kelly, Jane Fallowfield, Natasha Marshall, Vicky Featherstone, Jules Kelly, Tom Wells, Roy Alexander Weise, Jon Brittain and Balisha Karra for sharing your brilliant thoughts from your brilliant brains.

Philip and Christine Carne at The Carne Trust and Liz and Gordon Bloor at The Orseis Trust. Everyone at Nick Hern Books, Soho Writers' Alumni Group (SWAG), Theatr Clwyd, Gladstone's Library and Barnardo's.

To all the actors who contributed throughout the process including Corina Wilson, Gina Ruysen, Tripti Tripuraneni, Farshid Rokey, Danielle Bird, Nichole Bird, Fred Arnot, ALRA 2019 and 2020 graduating students.

And finally to the Wolfpack – Basia Bińkowska, Sara Malik, Belinda Chapman, Rose Hockaday, Richard Hammarton, Rajiv Pattani, Callum Finn, Paige Crimp, and to Erin Doherty and Sophie Melville for being fucking spectacular.

R.W.

WOLFIE

some sort of fairytale

Ross Willis

Characters

A
Z

A pair of twins. We meet them as unborn babies, thirteen and twenty-six years old.

Together they play:
NURSE
HUNGRY WOMAN
BONY MAN
SOGGY WOMAN
MA, *a wolf*
STRONTIUM, *a teacher*
PANTS
MANAGER
SPIDERS
PORCUPINE
SKUNK
TREES
WOODPECKER
MANNEQUIN MAN
INSANE MUM
SONOGRAPHER
FOETUS 1 *and* FOETUS 2 / BABY 1 *and* BABY 2
BRENDAS
BUTCHER

Notes on Text

This play should not be polite.

The entire auditorium should be the twins' playground. They should include the audience, sit, climb and play with the audience. Costumes should be left in the care of them and they should assist with costume changes. It should all feel very anarchic yet intimate and intensely personal but most importantly wild.

The dialogue switches between direct address and the internal world of the play.

The moments of magic should feel makeshift and created by the twins in the moment.

Scenes should bleed into one another.

If you wish to put in an intermission it should be placed between the second and third chapter.

A forward slash (/) denotes the playing of another character.

This text went to press before the end of rehearsals and so may differ slightly from the play as performed.

THE FIRST CHAPTER

Pre-Show

A pair of twin babies in their mother's womb.
A is raving to music. She is on it like a motherfucker.
Z is reading an encyclopedia, for the outside world is a scary place and she must be prepared.

One

Just a typical day for the TWINS *floating and chilling in the womb.*

A. Once upon a time we da Twins.

Z. We da Sharky Twins.
   First name Baby.
   Last name Sharky.

A. Winners of dat ultimate egg-and-spoon sperm race.
   Waitin for our victory lap.

Z. Kick.

A. Kick.

Z. We da Twins.

A. We da Sharky Twins.
   Queens of dis castle.
   Cuddle buddies for life.
   Got our futures all figured out.

Z. Got our futures all figured out.
   Secret language.

A. Hatin vegetables.
   We da Twins.

Z. We da Sharky Twins.

A. Gonna be born ten weeks too early!

Z. Wait what? –

A. We da Twins –

Z. We haven't discussed this.

A. I've made an executive decision.

Z. I'm not fully cooked yet.

A. Get your game face on yo.

Z. But it's cosy in here!

A. Five.
Four.

Z. My head isn't squishy enough!

A. THREE!!

Z. It's not time in da story!

A. Movin da story on!

Z. WAIT!

A. What!?

Z. Scared.

A. No.

Z. Don't.

A. Am.
I'll be wiv you.

Z. Don't let go.

A. Right now da old-ass sun is off her tits on heat.

Z. Right now dere is a Hungry Woman in a shop.

A. Our mum.

Z. Da Hungry Woman is countin pennies.
One penny.
Two penny.

A. Three penny.
   Four penny.
   Slams down a packet of Cup-a-Soup.

Z. Chicken flavour.

A. Good choice.
   Hungry Woman needs ninety pennies.
   Hands fumblin lookin to da floor.
   Self-service machine judgin her.
   Unexpected poverty in da baggin area.

Z. Hungry Woman ain't got ninety pennies.
   She ain't even close yo.
   Kick.

A. Kick.
   Men wiv hands full of pennies tuttin behind her.
   Tut.

Z. Tut.
   Suddenly dere is a gush.

A. A tsunami breakin from her.

Z. Pourin out of her.

A. Floodin da store.

Z. Drops da Cup-a-Soup.

A. Swept away by da waves.

Z. Sobbin covers up her rumblin stomach.

A. Poor Mummy Sharky.
   Winter babies shittin over her summer plans.
   Kick.

Z. Kick.

A. Layin on a hospital bed screamin on da hottest day of
   da year wasn't da plan.

Z. Her contractions contradict her.

A. Ice-cream truck jingle tryin to harmonise to her screams.

Z. STOP.

A. MOVE!

Z. CAN'T!

A. See you on da other side loser.

A *puts on a crash helmet and goggles and begins to be born.*

Ultimate road trip.
Cruisin down dat highway.
Car top open.
Wind in my hair.
Super slumber party over.
Twist and turn! Twist and turn!
Squeeze! Squeeze! Squeeze!

Z. Inhumane HOOOOOWLS!
Hungry Woman feelin like her spine is gonna snap snap snap away!

A. Floatin on a cloud of rainbows!

Z. Feelin like she's bein ripped ripped ripped apart by fire!

A. Floatin on a cloud of rainbows!
Twist and turn! Twist and turn!
Squeeze! Squeeze! Squeeze!

Z / NURSE. One last push!
You can do this!
ONE!

A. Fuzzy vision.

Z / NURSE. LAST!

A. Fuck me, it's cold!

Z / NURSE. PUSH!

A *is born.*
She and we the audience see the world for the first time.
It's an overwhelming sensory experience for her and it should be for the audience as well.

A. WOAAAAAAAAAH!
You gotta come out here yo!

Z. No!

A. DIS IS AMAZIN!
Yo, come on out or I'm draggin you out myself.

Hungry Woman has her eyes shut shut shut.
Hair like Cheesestrings coverin her face.

Z / HUNGRY WOMAN. Can't do this!

A / NURSE. Look at me Miss Sharky.
You *can* do this.
You are a Super Woman.

Z. Da Super Woman starts round two.

A. DING! DING!

Z. Sun knockin on da window tryin to get in.
Baby knockin on da door tryin to get out.

A. Da Super Woman is pushin.
Fightin against da pain in her body.
Fightin like she's had to fight her entire life.
She'll never get credit for dis moment.
Dis amazin moment.
Dis amazin Super Woman.
I see her and she is so beautiful.
She makes my heart sparkle and breathe glitter for her.
Like an inner light of love so bright
that the old-ass sun thinks we're comin for its job.

A sparkles and breathes glitter for her mum.
Z is born.
It's much less graceful. Actually frankly it's pretty fucking
messy.
Z then sparkles and breathes glitter for her mum. She mouths
'wow'.

Z. Dis feels amazin.

A. You took your fuckin time mate.
Nurse bring us to our Super Woman at once.

Z. Cuddle club here we come!

A. Our Super Woman shuts her eyes tight tight tight.
She can't see our sparkle.
Dis is all for you Mum.
Dis is love in motion.

Z. Why ain't she wavin back?

A. Why won't our Super Woman open her eyes?
   Eyes slammed shut.
   Shovin fingers into sockets.
   She's made a choice.

   A moment.

Z. Tryin to tell her that I love her.
   Words ain't comin out my mouth.
   Just baby gaga.

A. Dis was always her choice.

Z. She don't know us.

A. Our Super Woman might think she made da choice.

Z. Just one cuddle?

A. But dem tuttin men and countin pennies made da choice
   for her.
   And da old-ass sun don't fear our Super Woman's heart cuz
   it don't sparkle.
   We're bein taken away.

Z. Stop da story.

A. We da twins bein taken away from our Super Woman.

Z. Dis ain't how da story goes.

A. Da Febreze in her brain which should send out love ain't
   sprayin.

Z. Beggin her, just let us stay wiv you.
   Gotta make her open her eyes so she can see the sparkles.

A. We start high-fivin nurses.

Z. Dey love it yo.

A. Charmin charmin babies.

Z. Super Woman bein stubborn.
   We start dancin.

A. In perfect rhythm.

Z. Charmin charmin babies.

A. Baby boogie.

Z. Super Woman still bein stubborn.

A. We start jugglin live defibrillators.

Z. In perfect rhythm.

A. Charmin charmin babies.

Z. Dyin patients drag demselves out of bed to watch.

A. Standin ovation.
Charmin.

Z. Charmin.

A. Flies through me squidgy head straight to me squidgy brain.
Can't change destiny.
Babies can high-five, dance and juggle but dey can't change destiny.

Z. Don't say it.

A. And suddenly da story which we was gonna tell.

Z. Stop.

A. Da story which you was gonna listen.

Z. MUM!

A. Da story of da Sharky Twins is changed forever.

Two

The TWINS *take a moment to realise their story has been broken.*

A. Da Bony Man enters our story.

   Everything grinds to a halt a bit.

   …

Z. …

A. You be da Bony Man then.

Z. Na.

A. You gotta be da Bony Man!

Z. Fine.

A. Da Bony Man enters our story.

Z / BONY MAN. I'm ere for our babbas.

A. Da Bony Man.
    So skinny.
    Looks like he's in a constant battle wiv gravity to stand.

Z / BONY MAN. Where do I sign for our babbas?
    We had an *agreement*.

A. Yeah doesn't sound dodgy at all mate.
    He's thrown over a pen.

   *After a slight moment a pen is thrown from offstage or from
   the back of the audience.*

   Thanks.

Z / BONY MAN. It's fine I have my own pen.
    Actually, may I try yours?
    Oh what a lovely pen!

A. Da Bony Man shoves da pen into every crack and cranny of
    his mouth.

   Bony Man does this.

   Poor pen seein things no pen deserves to see.

   Signs da form.
   Takes da pen.
   Takes da babies.

   Afterwards Bony Man hands the pen to an audience member.

Three

The TWINS *create some sort of makeshift puppet bicycle and are placed in a bicycle basket.*
The cold night air blows through their bones.

A. We da Twins.

Z. We da Sharky Twins.

A. Bein pedalled away from our Super Woman.

Z. Lookin for da little lights in da black sky.
But da Bony Man has taken dem as well.

A. Younger sis be sobbin.
Bony feet be peddlin.

Z. YOUR FAULT!
IF WE HAD WAITED!

A. Don't.

Z. AM!

A. Please!

Z. No!
Babies and da Super Woman live happily ever after!
Dat was da story! Not dis story!
Don't want your story! Don't want you!

A. Sister makin boos boos.

Z. HATE YOUUUUUUUUUUUUUUUU!

A. Don't say dat.

Hug her tight.
Tryin to squeeze her shat-on heart back together.

Z. She never sparkled for us.
Not even one bit.

A. I sparkle for you.

Z. I never even knew what colour her eyes were.
What was dey?

A moment.

A. I never saw her eyes.
   Come on now get some sleep.

Z. Ain't tired.

A. You da ugly twin so you need your beauty sleep.

Z. You da ugly twin.

A. You gunna need to sleep forever to sort out dat face mate.

   And she laughs.
   And in dis moment I realise
   I wanna spend my entire life makin her laugh.

Z. Cuddles buddies for life?

A. Us against da world and baby poop on anyone else.

Z. And baby poop on anyone else.

A. She falls asleep quickly.
   As da old-ass sun fucks off for the night
   I see what was left of our childhood leave dis scary world.
   Best start pourin self-raisin flour ova us to raise ourselves.
   Bein a brave badass baby for sis but inside I am fuckin
   brickin it.

   Can I have a hug Mum?

   I need a hug.

   I really need a hug.

Four

Throughout the following, the TWINS *begin to build a sad-looking puppet together to be the Soggy Woman. Whatever they build should be slowly melting away from sadness.*

A. Right now da raindrops are smashin on da window bein
   a right diva.

Z. Right now dere is a Soggy Woman in a bath.

A. Cuz sometimes da Soggy Woman gets a lil sad.

Z. Soaks and shrivels in da bath for days.

A. Cus da men in white coats wiv clicky pens said it wasn't possible.

Z. Da men in white coats wiv clicky pens would go '*Aww I understand.*'

A. Like it was dem who had a uterus which wasn't workin.

Z. Thrown over a pamphlet wiv Comic Sans font.

A. 'How to be happy.'

Z. NEXT!

A. Right now dere is a Soggy Woman in da bath.

Z. Who gets a lil sad.

A. Soakin and shrivellin.

Z. Splash.

A. Splash.

> *The* TWINS *admire their handiwork.*

> You be da Bony Man again.

Z. Fuck's saaaaaaaake.

Z / BONY MAN. I've got a surprise for you my love! Something to finally make you smile.

A. We da twins bein carried up the stairs.

Z. One step.
Two steps.

A. Three steps.
Four steps.
Da Bony Man be wheezin.

Z. Gots to join a gym.

A. Five steps.
Six steps.

Z. Seven steps.
Eight steps.
We see da Soggy Woman in da bath.

A. We see da Soggy Woman in da bath.

Z. My new mother in da bath.

A. Dat's not my mother in da bath.
   Dat's a stranger danger in da bath.

Z. My new mother in da bath.

A. Baby head bein a killjoy thinkin somethin ain't right.
   Sister's head bein a cuddle addict thinkin everythin's alright.

Z. Baby fists be bumpin.
   Baby heart be thumpin.

Z / BONY MAN. I bought you something to make you smile
   my love.
   Now will you leave the bath?

A. And da Soggy Woman fights against dat sadness drippin
   from her.
   Looks to my sister.

Z. Stretches her eyes open and smiles.

A. Smiles a smile so big it don't fit in da bath.

Z. And da Bony Man realises
   all dem nights he spent wishin on dem little lights did
   real good.
   Eyes look over across to her.

A. Across to me.

Z. Across to her.

A. Across to me.
   Warm smile melts off her face.

Z. Drips into da bath.

A. Is it me?
   Am I ugly?
   I'll grow prettier with time.

Z / BONY MAN. Surprise!
   A second baby!
   We have twins!

A. Da Soggy Woman pushes her face back in da suds.

Z. Lets out a scream.

A. Like she's beggin da sky to fall in and crush her.

Z. Cuz she can barely love herself let alone two little lives.

The TWINS *scream at the top of their lungs.*

But wait.

A. What?

Z. Wait.

A. What?

Z. Wait.
Cuz suddenly da Bony Man lowers himself into da bath.

A. Past da suds.

Z. Past da icebergs.

A. Past da sadness.

Z. Straight to her heart.

A. Puts his ear next to it and listens to it beat beat beat.

Z. Like it's the prettiest song he has ever heard.

A. And suddenly for our Soggy Woman
dem single-glazed windows bought in da sale
feel like the safest thing in the world.

Z / BONY MAN. I won't let you drown in this water.
No matter how much you want to.
No matter how much you beg to.
I won't let you drown.

A. And he lifts us to her.

Z. Ever so gently.

A. Ever so gently.

Z. And places us in her soakin stiff arms

A. What the fuck is this wet stuff?

Z. I think I like it.

Z / BONY MAN. Will you not look?
They are beautiful.

A. We are pretty fuckin beautiful mate.

Z. Right now dere is a Soggy Woman in da bath.
Solemnly swearin that she will try to do what others find
so easy.

Z / BONY MAN. Your sparkle will come back.
Just you wait.
In three.
Two.

Five

Loud thumping music booms on. Fuckloads of movement.

A. Da months fuck on and on and on!
Right now we da Twins.

Z. Are full of unlimited wonder.

A. Shittin out unlimited wonder!

Z. Pissin out unlimited wonder!

A. From every fuckin orifice yo!

A. And da Bony Man just stares.

Z. WE SMASH THE FUCK OUT OF HEAD CONTROL.

*They should do movement for every new skill they learn.
They smash the fuck out of head control.*

A. WE SMASH THE FUCK OUT OF SMILIN!

They smash the fuck out of smiling.

Z. WE SMASH DA FUCK OUT OF SOLID FOODS!

They smash the fuck out of eating solid foods.

WE SMASH THE FUCK OUT OF DISTINGUISHIN
COLOURS.

They smash the fuck out of distinguishing colours.

A. CUSTARD YELLOW!

Z. ELECTRIC LIME!

A. While our Soggy Woman sinks away further each day.

The Soggy Woman begins melting away quicker and quicker.

Z / BONY MAN. My love the babies just wrote their first
symphony.
Will you not listen?

A. But da Soggy Woman just sinks lower in da suds.
A million drops of water ravin in her ears.

Z / BONY MAN. My love, the twins just wrote a bulletproof
plan to solve world hunger.
Will you not read it?

A. Da Soggy Woman just sinks lower in da suds.
Her heart bufferin bufferin bufferin.

Z / BONY MAN. My love, the twins just.

A. Here's where we wish we went:
Mate are you okay?
Let us help you?
Let us love you?

Z. Before it happens.
Before you let it happen.
But I was too busy bein distracted playin fuckin peekaboo.

A. In your defence it's a very witty game.

Z. I guess so.

Here it is.
Da shit bit.

A. Da shit bit.

Z / BONY MAN. My love, will you not look!?
Will you not try!?
Tell me what I must do to make you happy!?

A. And wiv her soggy hands and soggy heart.

Z. Da Soggy Woman makes a tear in our story.

A. Sayin da unthinkable with a tiny whisper.

Z. So dem big comets in the sky won't hear her and tut.

A *and* Z / SOGGY WOMAN. 'If you took a twin away…'

'Maybe I could try.'

Z. Tell her no Bony Man!

A. We hear the sounds of the wanky water drippin.
Drip.

Z. Drop.
And as it hits this loveless floor it sounds like it's mockin us.

A. Like it's sayin you actually thought you were safe here?
You thought you were wanted?
You thought they would put your needs before theirs?

Z. Drip

A. Drop.

Z. You will never feel safe.
You will never feel wanted.
You will never have your needs put first.

A. Drip

Z. Drop.

A. Drip

Z. Drop.

Z / BONY MAN. If it shall make your heart sparkle again
I shall take one away to the woods.
Bring my gun
and shoot her dead so she may never return.

A. Suddenly da bony hands swoop me up!

Z. Please!

A. Say it.

Z / BONY MAN. I'M KEEPING YOU BOTH!

A. He never said dat mate.

Z / BONY MAN. We're going for a walk in the woods little one.

A. Dat's right.

Z. Please?

A. And?

Z. Don't want.

A. Tell the story!

Z / BONY MAN. I'll make it quick little one.

A. And he looks at me.

Z. And he looks at you.

A. Like I'm his.

A moment.

As the TWINS *are split up the earth cracks open. Absolute chaos.*

AND SUDDENLY DA STORY OF DA SHARKY TWINS. DA STORY WHICH WE WAS GONNA TELL.

Z. DA STORY WHICH YOU WAS GONNA LISTEN.

A. IS.

Z. TORN.

A. IN.

Z. TWO.

Six

A. Da Bony Man and da baby
in da deep dark woods.
Goin for a stroll
in da deep dark woods.
Murderin da baby
in da deep dark woods.
In da deep dark woods.
In da deep dark woods.

Fuckloads of trees
in da deep dark woods.

But da trees don't give a shit
in da deep dark woods.
Cuz da trees seen many murders
in da deep dark woods.
In da deep dark woods.
In da deep dark woods.

Da Bony Man holdin me tight in his bony hands
like a father?
My father places me on da ground.
My father aims his gun at me.
Bye sky.
Bye ground.
Da trees put in dere earplugs.
Da bony mouth apologises to da moon for what it's about
to see.
Da gun barrel crushes my soft spot.

Z / BONY MAN. My heart would have sparkled for you with
all the glitter in this world.

A. Baby cold.
Baby hungry.
Baby wants to live!

Bony Man drops a seed on the ground.

Z / BONY MAN. If you take a life out you give a life back.

A. Baby heart breakin.
Baby head shakin.
Tryin to tell him no.
But just gurgle wah!
Gurgle wah!
Fuck!
PLEASE!

Bony finger on da trigger.

And I'm thinkin about my sista wiv her head full of hugs.
And I'm thinkin about my sista wiv her head full of hugs.

Murderin da baby.
In da deep dark woods!
In da deep dark woods!
In da deep dark –

Never lose your sparkle sis.
That's all I want.

Just please
never lose your sparkle.

Bony Man is about to shoot. A wolf (Ma) appears and rips
Bony Man into a thousand tiny pieces.
The TWINS *should enjoy this makeshift set-piece.*
Z suddenly flicks the lights off.

THE SECOND CHAPTER

One

Z. Can we stop?

A. We need to tell the story.

　A *flicks the lights on.*

Z. Let's go back to the beginnin.

A. We can't keep doin the beginnin.

Z. We da Twins!
We da Sharky Twins!

A. Tell the story!
Do you wanna go first?

Z. You go first.

A. You go first.

Z. You go first.

A. You go first.

Z. I know you like to go first.

A. I don't like to go first.

　Z *begins to speak.*

　Actually I'll go first.

Two

Thirteen years later.

Loud music blasts on. A giant neon tree begins to grow from the earth from where the seed was dropped.

A *transforms into a feral child raised by a wolf in front of our eyes. Fuckloads of movement. She is animalistic and wild. She frantically moves like she's filling the entire space with her body. She rubs blood all over her face and mud all over her body. She licks the audience's faces.*

A wolf (Ma) enters the den. She is much less of a tryhard and simply puts on a fabulous fur coat and maybe a tiny bit of blood and mud. She's getting ready for a big night out.

Z / MA. Stay in the den!

A. Ma! Pleeeease! PLEEEEEEASE!

Z / MA. Stay in the den!
GRRRRRRRRR!

A. *AWOOOOOOOOOOOOOO!!*
Yous hate me!

Z / MA. Go play with that little lad raised by squirrels.

A. He's not here any more Ma.

Z / MA. Go play with the trees.

A. The trees hate me Ma!

Z / MA. They don't hate yous!
The trees love all hoooomaaan children of these woods.

A. THEY HATE ME!
They say your heart never sparkles for me!
I hear them whisper things about the way I look.

Z / MA. Yous look beautiful baby.

A. I'd look more beautiful HUUUUNTIN! I'd keep up!

Z / MA. You're not ready baby.

A. Yous hate me!

Z / MA. I don't hate yous baby.

A. YOUS HATE ME!

> Ma is hypin herself up.
> Gettin ready to hunt.
> Tail high.
> Bares teeth.
> Claws sharp.
> Stands tall.

MA! PLEASE! PLEEEEEASE!

> And she licks my face.
> Warm.
> Wet.
> Nice.
> Home.

LEMMMME COME!

Z / MA. I can't carry yous when huntin baby.

A. FUCK'S SAAAAAAKE! *GRRRRRRRRR!!!!*

> And she stands there
> lookin all serious until she gently nibbles my arm.

Z / MA. YOUR FACE!

A. WHAT! NAH! NAH! NAH! WHAT!

Z / MA. OF COURSE yous comin huntin!

A. YES MA!
AWOOOOOOOOOOOOOO!!

Z / MA. Make a good impression okay? First hunt is important.

A. Snuggle up to her.
> Place my tongue on her fur.
> Warm.
> Wet.
> Nice.
> Home.

Z / MA. Get ready little one.
TAIL HIGH!

A. Tail High!

Z / MA. BARE TEETH!

A. Bare Teeth!

Z / MA. CLAWS SHARP!

A. Claws Sharp!

Z / MA. STAND TALL!

A. Stand Tall!

Z / MA. Check yous out!
What a babe! That's my little predator!

A. DO I LOOK GOOD MA? DO I LOOK GOOD!?

Z / MA. Good!? Yous look FUCKIN STUNNIN baby!
AWOOOOOOOOOOOOOOOOOOOOOOOOOO!!

A. *AWOOOOOOOOOOOOOOOOOOOOOOOOOO!!*

Z / MA. Are yous ready little one?
Cuz now
we hunt.

Three

Z. MY TURN!

A. WHAT!

Z. MY TURN!

Z is in detention in a science lab with her science teacher Strontium.

Actually there's an art form to flushin someone's head down the toilet.

A / STRONTIUM. Well done you.

Z. I'm pissed off you haven't complimented me but whatever.

A / STRONTIUM. She's upset.

Z. That was the intention.

A / STRONTIUM. Why did you do it?

Z. Made fun of my shoes.

A / STRONTIUM. If I made fun of your shoes would you flush
    my head down the toilet?

Z. Yup.

A / STRONTIUM. You're a bright girl Francium.
    You have an understanding of chemistry way beyond
    your years.

Z. Miss calls me Francium
    cuz it's so radioactive
    that it tends to dissolve itself before it has a chance to do
    anythin.
    It's its own worst enemy.
    And it's rare.
    Really rare.

A. Can we go back to me now?

Z. Nope.

    I call her Strontium.
    It's the chemical which gives fireworks their red colour
    and she always wears the same old shitty red jumper.

    How long left Strontium?

A / STRONTIUM. About ten minutes.
    I think we have enough time for a quick experiment.
    Francium is everything okay at home?

Z. I put my safety goggles on cuz I can't look her in the eyes.

A / STRONTIUM. Don't tell anyone I shown you this.

Z. This is my favourite part of detentions with Strontium.
    When she starts pokin my brain.

A / STRONTIUM. I mean it.

Z. She gets out a tiny bottle of pig's blood and some hydrogen
    peroxide.
    And ever so precisely like an artist
    Strontium releases three drops of pig's blood into the
    hydrogen peroxide.
    And what happens next is beautiful.
    Bubbles upon bubbles upon bubbles.

Alterin the very composition of the blood.
Alterin my mind.
And in this moment.

I realise

this.

This is what I wanna do with my life.

A / STRONTIUM. It's the blood that's the catalyst.
Of course, you already knew that.

Z. I already knew that.
But when Strontium speaks
she makes me feel like
I can push back all the gravity in this world and float into
space.

Like I could just reach out and touch all the little lights in
the sky.

Maybe that's what life is about?
Findin the people who make you feel like you can push back
gravity?

Sometimes I feel my heart sparklin for her.

Z begins to sparkle but stops herself.

But I gotta hide it cuz she's a teacher, she's not my mum.

I wish she was my mum.

Cuz this is my favourite part of the story.
Chemistry with Strontium.
And as twattin time carries on I beg it to stay.

A / STRONTIUM. Time's up you're a free woman.

Z. Strontium, don't tell my mum I was in detention?

A / STRONTIUM. Francium, I never have and I never will.
Is everything okay at home?

Z. Do really think I'm smart?

A / STRONTIUM. I would bet all the Poudretteite in the world
on it.

Four

A. MY TURN!

Z. I was just gettin goin!

A. MY TURN!

Fuckloads of movement.

AND THEN WE ARE RUNNIN.
WE THE WOLVES.
RUNNIN.
ME AND MA.
RUNNIN.

Z / MA. IN THE DEEP DARK WOODS.

A. IN THE DEEP DARK WOODS.
AWOOOOOOOOOOOOOOOO!!!

Ma out front.

So black.
So fast.
So dope.
So dark.

Little lights gone on holiday.
Barbershop quartet of crickets.
Crunchy leaf beat booms.
Cold wind yos BRRRRR bitches.

Z / MA. Can yous smell that baby?

A. Snout sniffin scent.
Can't smell anythin.
Can't tell her that.

Z / MA. That's our dinner!

A. WE ARE HUNTIN.

Z / MA. IN THE DEEP DARK WOODS!

A. IN THE DEEP DARK WOODS!
And it's like the first time I see Ma as not just Ma.
Who feeds me.
Who licks me.
Who cuddles me.

These are her woods.
She's a fuckin boss yo.

Savage.
Vicious.
Graceful.
Beauty.

And then we see em from behind.

Their behinds.
Moose booty.
Our dinner.
CUZ WE IS HUNTIN.

Z / MA. IN THE DEEP DARK WOODS.

A. IN THE DEEP DARK WOODS.

Z / MA. Come on keep up now baby.

A. Heart races.
Mouth pants.
Sweat pours.

Trees laughin throwin shade.
Ma's eyes throwin love.
Sayin yous can do this.
Her sparkle lightin my way in the darkness.

TAIL HIGH!
BARE TEETH!
CLAWS SHARP!
STAND TALL!

WATCH ME FUCKIN GO!
YOUS WATCHIN YEAH?
Oi Ma! Ma! YOUS WATCHIN?

Z / MA. THEY'RE GETTIN AWAY!

A. NAH! NAH! NAAAAAAH!

They play with an audience member.

And we see the moose we want.

Z / MA. A basic bitch.

A. A little jiggly twat.

Z / MA. Strugglin.

A. Panickin.

Z / MA. Fallin.

A. So we separate the little jiggly twat from her ma.
And I'm thinkin
SHE LOOKS TASTY I'LL AVE A BIT OF THAT.
And Ma is thinkin.

Z / MA. YEAH SHE LOOKS TASTY I'LL AVE A BIT OF
THAT!

A. She turns.

Z / MA. So we turn.

A. AND SHE TURNS.

Z / MA. SO WE TURN.

A. Oi where ya goin babe?
Just wanna chat yo.

Z / MA. Faster!

A. TAIL HIGH!

Z / MA. Faster!

A. BARE TEETH!

Z / MA. Faster!

A. CLAWS SHARP!

Z / MA. Faster!

A. STAND TALL!

Z / MA. IN FOR THE KILL BABY!

A. *GRRRRRRRRRRRRRRRRRRRRRRRRRRRR!!!!*
AND I SOAR PAST MA!
Trees wide-mouthed.
Squirrels Mexican wave.
Gravity can fuck right off.
Cuz me and Ma pushed it back.
She is so proud.

Z / MA. THAT'S MY LITTLE PREDATOR!!!!

A. And then it's just.
BITE DOWN.
SQUEEZE.
ALL TOGETHER.

Z / MA. BITE DOWN.
SQUEEZE.
ALL TOGETHER.

A. BITE DOWN.
SQUEEZE.
But then I remember I hadn't thought about my sister once today.

Z / MA. NO BABY NO!

A. So I stop.
Ma carries on and I see her disappointed eyes starin back.

I do what I do every night
I try to remember everythin I can about my little sister.

Her blue eyes.
Her delicate skin.
Her beautiful laugh.

And I wonder
what does your laugh sound like now?
What do you look like?
Are you forgettin me?

Z. No.

A. Have you forgotten me?

Z. Yes.

Five

Z. My mum, the Soggy Woman in the bath
has days where I can feel her heart beatin for me out her chest.
And days where she sinks under the heavy water.
Rages at the old-ass sun for havin the audacity to even shine.
Cuz when her Bony Man fucked off this mortal coil.
Soggy Woman's heart cracked into a million soggy pieces.
Fell straight down the plughole.

Can we skip ahead?

A. We need to tell your story.

Z. What if they judge me? That person has judgy eyes.

A looks.

A. Fuckin hell you do have judgy eyes. Maybe just shut them?

We see the Soggy Woman again. Z is trying everything she can to keep her together but she is slipping through her fingers. Z looks at the Soggy Woman in the most loving way any human has ever looked at anything.

Z. My Soggy Woman in the bath.
Wet and wrinkly in the bath.
Beauty evaporated in the bath.

As a child, I learned how to say I love you in twenty different languages
hopin one of them would fix the chemical imbalance in her brain.
Drew a billion drawins of her smilin just so I could finally see it.

I put my hand in the water.
Ice cold.
I gently pull out the plug and refill the bath.

I put on 'Girls Just Want to Have Fun' cuz she likes that song.
And just like Strontium showed me.
I put on my goggles.
I get the chemicals I stole from her supply cupboard.
I add milk, vanilla, protein powder to liquid nitrogen
and make ice cream to feed her
and when the room gets a chill
I mix aluminium with iron oxide and sit by the flame.

Will you stay?
Will you stay a little longer?
Cuz I'd like to get to know you.
And maybe you'd like to get to know me?

As my Soggy Woman lowers her head back in the bath.
I pretend I can hear her say I love you through the bubbles
and I keep my goggles on so she can't see me cry.

(*In French.*) I love you.
(*In German.*) I love you.
(*In Italian.*) I love you.

Z sparkles and breathes out glitter for the Soggy Woman.
She sits and waits for the Soggy Woman to do the same.
She will be waiting forever.

Six

A. Ma sleeps.
   Back turned.
   Ears down.
   Heart beats.

   Yous mad at me Ma?

Z / MA. Daytime.
   Sleep baby.

A. And she squeezes me tight
   like she's tryin to squeeze her way into my dreams
   and me and Ma lay in one big cuddle puddle in her winter
   coat of wonder.
   We sparkle so brightly we coat the planets in glitter.

Z / MA. Snuggle up.
   Eyes shut.
   Dream big.

A. Ma tell me a story!

Z / MA. The bumblebees have just taken in a new baby boy.
   I don't wanna wake him.

A. AWWWWWWWWWW Ma tell me a story!

And she lays there lookin all serious until she gently nibbles my arm.

Z / MA. YOUR FACE! I GOT YOUS!

A. WHAT! NAH! NAH! NAH! WHAT!

Z / MA. Course I'll tell yous a story.

Now yous know when every livin thing loves they sparkle from within.
Cuz once a upon a fuckin time when our world was born the first little light in the night sky fell in love with the second little light.
But no such words of love had been created yet.
So they sparkled for each other from afar.
Glitter lit a freshly made sky
waitin for a new world to catch up.

A. And then we go to sleep and that's where this part of the story ends. Night!

Z. That's not what happened.

A. NIGHT!

Z. You said we can't change the story!

A. You're obviously the evil twin!

Z. Say it.

A. No!

Z leaps on top of A and playfully attacks her to make her tell the story properly.

OKAY OKAY!

'Me and yous Ma we're gonna hunt the moon forever.'

And as soon as I say it

I wish I didn't.

It's like

her heart is leakin out on the den floor.

Z / MA. No baby.
One day you're gonna age out and have to leave the woods.

A. But you're my ma?

Z / MA. The Woodpecker will arrive and take yous to live in the
hoooomaaan world.
It happens to all hoooomaaan children of these woods.

It doesn't seem fair but it's all we got.

You're mine but only mine for a moment.

A. Does your heart not sparkle for me?

Z / MA. Not for a long time though baby!
Now snuggle up.

A. Snuggle up.

Z / MA. Eyes shut.

A. Eyes shut.

Z / MA. Dream big.

A. Dream big!!

Z / MA. Promise me somethin baby?

A. Anythin Ma.

Z / MA. Never age out.

A. And I push my toesies into the ground to try and make
myself stop growin.
And as I do
I feel drops of water hit my head like when the sky cries.
But they're comin from Ma.

Seven

The Soggy Woman is melting away faster and faster. Z is unable to help her yet continues to sparkle for her.

A. She's gettin worse.

Z. She's gettin better.

A. Why do you keep comin back?

Z. I pull out the plug and refill the bath and she's gettin better.
I put on 'Girls Just Want to Have Fun' and she's gettin better.
I add milk, vanilla, protein powder to liquid nitrogen...

Z looks at the Soggy Woman melting away and allows herself one painful moment of realisation that she isn't getting better.

School was good today Mum.
Strontium taught me how
one bucketfull of water contains more atoms
than there are buckets of water in the entire Atlantic ocean.

Does that not make you love this world?

Mum please?

I just want to be your daughter.

One of the girls said I smelled today so I punched her.

I need you to wash my clothes please Mum.
Will you wash my clothes please?

I'd make the detergent myself
but if I steal all of Strontium's supplies she's gonna notice ain't she?

I need clean pants Mum.

Help me?
I turned them inside out cuz I didn't wanna bother you
but I can't turn them inside out any more.

Mum I stink.
I fuckin stink.

Will you wash my pants Mum?
Please?

Just do this one thing for me?
You don't need to sparkle,
just be my mum and wash my pants?

Z silently begs the Soggy Woman. A can't bear to watch any more so she begins to operate Soggy Woman. Z stares in wonder at Soggy Woman.

A / SOGGY WOMAN. Okay honey. I'll do it straight away.

Z. She never said that.

A / SOGGY WOMAN. And my heart will sparkle so brightly for you.

Z. You're changin the story.

A / SOGGY WOMAN. That all the light from this world will bow down and retire.

Z continues to stare in wonder. She finally snaps herself out of it.

Z. I leave the house and go to the shop.
Straight to the pants section.
As I'm lookin at them all I realise I got no money on me.
Only thing I got on me is dirty pants.

I pick up a pack of unicorn pants.
There's a unicorn on each one doin a different activity
and the unicorn looks really happy to be doin it.

A puts on a unicorn horn and becomes the Pants. She does whatever activity the unicorn on the pants is doing.

A / PANTS. DANCING UNICORN!!

Z. I wanna feel clean.

A / PANTS. ASTRONAUT UNICORN!!

Z. I wanna feel like every other kid.

A / PANTS. BUSINESS ANALYST UNICORN!!

Z. I put the pants up my jumper and I run as fast as I can.
I hear all the pants down the aisle screamin.

A / PANTS. SHAME ON YOU!

Z. I'm so close to the exit.

A / PANTS. You keep running.
I'll blow up security with my jellybean bombs.

Dancing Unicorn, don't help her!

It's okay for you Business Analyst Unicorn, you've got
a career!
The only thing I do is dance!

Z. But as I'm runnin a security guard stops me.

Eight

A. MY TURN!

Z. Hey I hadn't finished!

A. Yeah you have.

Z. Bitch.

A. CUZ WE IS HUNTIN!
IN THE DEEP DARK WOODS!

Fuckloads of movement again.

Z / MA. Baby slow down!

A. And the spiders say.

Z / SPIDERS. Look at her go!
Look at her go!
Look at her go!

A. And they all high-five me eight times each like.

Z / SPIDERS. LEGEND!
LEGEND!
LEGEND!

A. And the porcupine says.

Z / PORCUPINE. My my little one, aren't you growing up fast?

A. And the skunk says.

Z / SKUNK. I could sell you somethin to stop you growin mate?

A. And the trees say.

Z / DORIS THE TREE. We the trees of these woods watched the sky be made.

Z / PHYLLIS THE TREE. We watched the water wet itself.

Z / ETHEL THE TREE. We watched the cloud of gas roar itself into a sun.

Z / DORIS THE TREE. And now we're doing admin!

A. Come play?

Z / ETHEL THE TREE. Someone pass me my earplugs.
Back to work ladies.
We have so many more hoooomaaans to home.

A. Come play!

Z / ETHEL THE TREE. Go away hoooomaaan!
Back in the day you could just fall down and crush them to death.

Z / DORIS THE TREE. Can we place this hoooomaaan with the slugs?

Z / PHYLLIS THE TREE. Let's place this hoooomaaan with the pigeons?

Z / ETHEL THE TREE. Could this hoooomaaan be placed with the eels?

A. Come play!

Z / DORIS THE TREE. We the trees of these woods watched the sky be made.

Z / PHYLLIS THE TREE. We watched the water wet itself.

Z / ETHEL THE TREE. We watched the cloud of gas roar itself into a sun.

Z / DORIS THE TREE. We don't play.

Z / AMY THE SAPLING. I play! Weeeeeeeeeee!!

Z / DORIS THE TREE. Phyllis, what is your sapling doing here?

Z / PHYLLIS THE TREE. Sorry Doris it's Bring Your Sapling to Work Day.
Sweetie, just sit in the corner and grow quietly.

Z / AMY THE SAPLING. 'WE THE CHEESE OF THESE WORLDS WATCHED THE PIES BE MADE!'

Z / DORIS THE TREE. Phyllis, your sapling is off her fucking head on nitrogen.
How are we supposed to get any work done?

Z / AMY THE SAPLING. Ohmygod I love you guys! I love you!

Z / ETHEL THE TREE. Back to work ladies.
So many more hoooomaaans to home.

Amy, small sips of nitrogen.
Not big ones.
You're drunk off your tits love.
Also pay attention because you'll be doing this when you're older.

Z / AMY THE SAPLING. I'm gonna move to Cornwall and become a famous postcard!

Z / ETHEL THE TREE. Back to work ladies.
Let's place this hoooomaaan with the arachnids?

Z / DORIS THE TREE. Let's place this hoooomaaan with the stingrays?

Z / PHYLLIS THE TREE. Can we place this hoooomaaan with the fungus?

Z / AMY THE SAPLING. OhMyGod Brad the Stinging Nettle is soooo cute!
He's really prickly and evil but I could change him.
I. Could. Change. Him.

A. Is no one goin to play with me?

Z / DORIS THE TREE. Go away hoooomaaan!
We have so much work to do!
Back in the day it was fine
We would only take in one or two hoooomaaans.
There was enough oxygen and shelter to go around.
But now there's so many.

Z / ETHEL THE TREE. Back to work ladies.
Have we heard back from the fungus yet?
Everyone has to do their duty.

A. Duty?
My ma's heart sparkles for me and mine sparkles for her.
I see it fill the night sky.

Z / DORIS THE TREE. You're just another hoooomaaan child
counting off time
until the Woodpecker arrives.
Isn't she Phyllis?

Z / PHYLLIS THE TREE. Yes Doris.
She's just another hoooomaaan child counting off time
until the Woodpecker arrives.
Isn't that right Ethel?

Z / ETHEL THE TREE. Yes Phyllis.
She's just another hoooomaaan child counting off time
until

Nine

Z. I'm not playin every fuckin tree!

The manager's office is full of inspirational quotes.

A. I Never Dreamed About Success I Worked for It.

Z. He has them stapled everywhere.

A. Believe. Achieve. Succeed.

Z. He's the type of man
who in twenty years time will be sobbin in the cheese aisle
of Co-op.

He circles the office like he's tryin to show it off to me.
Like if I can change my ways, maybe I can be him one day.
Picks up a paper shredder.

A / MANAGER. John Lewis.
Not a Christmas present, didn't even have a voucher.
Just bought it myself because I could.

Z. He sits down and taps the desk four times.

A / MANAGER. Tap.

Z. Tap.

A / MANAGER. Tap.

Z. Tap.

A / MANAGER. So hun.

Z. He overarticulates the word hun.

A / MANAGER. HUN!

Z. Why is he callin me hun?

A / MANAGER. Are you part of a gang HUN!?

Z. Nah.

A / MANAGER. Have they made you steal these pants HUN!?

Z. I'm sorry alright.

A / MANAGER. HUN! I'm not one to judge.

Z. And then he judges me.
Looks at me like I'm a piece of.

A / MANAGER. Shit.

Z. Like I'm.

A / MANAGER. Evil.

Z. I wanna tell him, I just wanted to feel clean like you.
I wanted to know what it must be like to have a mum who
loves you.
But him thinkin I'm a piece of shit is better than him knowin
the truth.

A / MANAGER. I worked all my life and never stole from
anyone HUN!
As soon as I left public school I worked at my dad's company.

Z. ...

A / MANAGER. I can see I'm not getting through to your evil brain.
Maybe I'll get through to your parents?

Z. Please don't.

A / MANAGER. Either you give me their number or I'm calling the police.

Z. I give him the only number I know.
He goes into the hallway and makes a phone call.

A / MANAGER. Comes back for the John Lewis paper shredder.
Didn't even have a voucher, just bought it myself.

Z. And I'm wishin I had some lithium and water to blast myself out of here.
He returns and taps the desk four times.

A / MANAGER. Tap.

Z. Tap.

A / MANAGER. Tap.

Z. Tap.
And she comes. She actually comes.
Strontium with her face redder than her jumper.

Ten

A *has her first period. She is terrified.*

A. No one was exactly sure when it started.

Z. Not the moon.

A. Or the ants.

Z. The moon said she couldn't quite see what was goin on but even she heard the screams way up there.

A. The ants were annoyed.

Z. Rightly so.

A. They had just cleaned the ground and now it's bein bled on.
Bit selfish.

Z. Ma's eyes drippin sadness, always knew this horrible human
day would come.

A. MA HELP ME!

Z. Ma tries to lick up the blood.

A. Hide it under the rug but the trees have seen it ain't they.

Z / MA. Run back to the den and don't let any more trees see
you bleed!

A. The trees start shakin each other's branches.
Like they actually partook in the raisin of this child.
Like they aren't about to partake in the throwin-out of
this child.

Z / MA. For once in your life just listen!

A. Am I gonna be okay Ma?

Z / MA. No baby, you're not.

Eleven

Z. Can you tell when a parent loves you?

A / STRONTIUM. Now isn't the time to be changing the subject.
Talk to me about the unicorn pants.

Z. Like scientifically, can you tell?

A / STRONTIUM. That number was for emergency purposes.

Z. I don't think my mum loves me Strontium.

A / STRONTIUM. That's not true Francium.

Z. I don't think she's ever loved me.
How am I gonna grow if I'm not loved?

A / STRONTIUM. Who couldn't love that brain of yours
Francium?
Even if you have become a kleptomaniac.

Z. Nobody loves me.

I don't want to be a scientist any more.

Twelve

Ma is running against the rising sun, wind and falling leaves to beg for her child to stay.

Z / MA. She isn't ready to leave!
She knows nothin of the hoooomaaan world!

A / CORA THE TREE. The hoooomaaan has aged out and now must leave.
INDEPENDENT HOOOOMAAAN LIVING!

Z / MA. Give me one more sunrise!?

A / CORA THE TREE. Furry parent of our woods you cannot just demand things!

A / MABEL THE TREE. Totally fucking agree Cora. I demand she shuts up!

A / RITA THE TREE. What if everyone started demanding things!?
What if the worms demanded to move faster? Eh Cora?

A / CORA THE TREE. You're right Rita. Or the fish demanded to live in the sky?

A / MABEL THE TREE. Or the clouds demanded to be predators?

A / RITA THE TREE. Yes Mabel, or the badgers demanded to fly?

A. That's it, I'm not playin every tree.

Z / MA. Edna will yous not help me!?
You're the oldest tree of these woods.
You've seen every sparkle of love.
Every glitter of love fall upon your ground.

A. ...

Z. ...

A. ...

A / EDNA THE TREE. The furry parent is right.

I remember when I was a seedling how much I needed the
ground to feed me.

A child of the woods.
A little hoooomaaan boy.
A dirty little adorable boy.

His mother was found dead by Agatha's stump.

Does anyone remember Agatha?
She was turned into a pamphlet.

When we found him the little boy was alone.
So we raised him like our own.

Being a parent was never about the act of bearing a child.
It was about bearing witness to a life.

But one day he got too tall.
Aged out.
So we ripped him from our ground and he had to leave.

My boy.
My boy.
My dirty little adorable boy.

If I was plucked from this ground as a seedling would I have
survived?
Would any of us have survived?

I am afraid of what will happen to these children
if no one took the risk to love them.

But I am more afraid of what happens to them after.

We the trees of these woods failing.

Failing the children.
Failing the seeds.
Failing the future.

If the sky dropped the stars or the river drained the water
there would be outrage.

But we treat children like this and there is silence.

I should beg the sun to give you a million more sunrises.

But I cannot.

Or perhaps I just do not.

So I just hang my branches in shame.

And hope when the thunder spits and strikes it does not miss me.

Back in the den. Ma looks at her daughter and sparkles for her.

A. My tummy hurts.

Z / MA. Just rest baby.

A. Are we goin huntin tomorrow?

Z / MA. The trees say you're a grown-up now and have to leave.

A. I don't feel like a grown-up.

Z / MA. I need yous to know I tried.
This isn't a system built for love or young things
but I tried with all the try I had.

On your first night in the woods all the little lights were glowin.
It was like they were glowin just for you.

Keep glowin for her.

Let her live a life of never-endin light.

Ma places her sparkle in A's hands as a keepsake.
Ma then takes off the fur coat for the final time and leaves the den. A howls for her to return.

Thirteen

A *looks over to the fur coat. Z looks to the Soggy Woman.*
They sing a song and for a moment both are perfectly
connected.

Fourteen

The Soggy Woman is melting away faster and faster. Z is done
caring.

Z. There's a rage in me tonight.
   Like a gummy bear chucked in potassium chlorate.
   A big fuckin exothermic reaction explodin out of me.
   But even a gummy bear has other gummy bears who care
   about him.

   I check on Mum.
   Always checkin on Mum.
   Forever checkin on Mum.
   No one checks on me but I check on Mum.

   I never realised how ugly she is.
   Flesh bloated with soapy water.

   I put on 'Girls Just Want to Have Fun' cuz she liked that
   song once.

   I add milk, vanilla and protein powder to liquid nitrogen
   and make ice cream to feed her

   and

   I

   She takes a moment to make a decision.

   I have sparkled for you every single day.

   What is in your mouth where your sparkles should be?
   Did the water dampen your glitter or was it just never in you
   in the first place?

   She takes another moment to make a decision.

I turn on the cold water.
It charges into the bath.
Stings her flesh and spills over the side.

A. You can stop this.

Z. If you sparkle for me I'll turn it off.
Just one bit of sparkle!

A. STOP!

Z. I open all the windows.
Let the wind see how ugly she is.
And it blows through her cracklin damp skin.

Will you not sparkle!? Do you hate me this much Mum!?

Then I'll tip in some hydrofluoric acid
and turn your rottin cells into dead tissues!

A. ENOUGH!

A *takes the Soggy Woman from her.*

Fifteen

A *sits alone still howling for Ma. The den begins to crumble.*
The Woodpecker flies into the den.

Z / WOODPECKER. The Woodpecker Has Arrived! Peck.
Peck. Peck.
INDEPENDENT HOOOOMAAAN LIVING!

Former child of the woods. Peck.
Hoooomaaan adult raised by wolf. Peck.
Your aged-out head closer to the sun.
Your aged-out legs further from the ground.
Your aged-out blood floods our woods. Peck. Peck. Peck.

A. Where am I to go!?

Z / WOODPECKER. Anywhere that's not here hoooomaaan.
Peck. Peck. Peck.

A. This is my home!

Z / WOODPECKER. This is not your home any more
hoooomaaan.
It is time to leave. Peck. Peck. Peck.

A. Make the story stop!

Z / WOODPECKER. You were a child of the woods.
This day is your very birthright.
It is the predator and you are the prey
and has been chasing you since the day you arrived.
But you cannot outrun this.
It has gobbled you up.
Now hold on to my beautiful wing! Peck. Peck. Peck.

A *and Woodpecker fly out of the den across the woods.
Fuckloads of movement.*

UP UP UP WE GO.
Stop crying, you're making my beautiful wing wet.

A. I'm sorry!

Z / WOODPECKER. Down in the bricks is where the
hoooomaaans live. Peck. Peck. Peck.

A. I don't know those bricks Woodpecker.

Z / WOODPECKER. I shall visit you from time to time to
check you are integrating.
The trees want you to do well.
I want you to do well.
We all want you to do well.

Okay I'm going to drop you now.

A. What!?

Z / WOODPECKER. I'm going to drop you.

A. I'm not prepared for this!

Z / WOODPECKER. That is not our concern.
You have been raised and now you must go be a hoooomaaan.
Peck. Peck. Peck.

A. You never taught me how!

Z / WOODPECKER. Peckidy-fuckin-Peck-Peck! I do not have
the time for this!

A. I feel the sparkles leavin me.

Z / WOODPECKER. I warned you I'm going to drop you.

A. Floatin away in the night sky.

Z / WOODPECKER. Please try to land on your feet, not your head.

A. Help!

Z / WOODPECKER. If you land on your head you will die.

A. Help!

Z / WOODPECKER. So please try to land on your feet.

A. Help!

Z / WOODPECKER. A lot of hoooomaaans land on their heads and die.

A. Help!

Z / WOODPECKER. They're just not trying hard enough to integrate.

The Woodpecker drops A.

INDEPENDENT HOOOOMAAAN LIVING!

A *falls and begins to lose her sparkle.*

Z. I look out the window and see all the little lights in the sky.

And the sky is spittin thunder sayin don't do this girl.

So I reply.

Little lights in the sky!

I do not want this sparkle!
I do not want this glitter!
I do not want this love!

A. Someone catch me!
I beg you ground!
I beg you world!
Please someone catch me!

Z. It is no use to me!
   It has never been any use to me!
   Take it back!
   Will you not take it back!?

A. I look up cuz I can't look down.
   And I see woodpeckers droppin children from the sky!
   Hundreds and hundreds of children!
   Absolute fear leakin from their eyes!
   Fallin!
   Beggin!
   Screamin!

Z. Then I'll rip out the sparkles from my flesh myself and I'll
   puke up the glitter!

A. Fingernails clingin on to planets and clouds!
   Sparkles and light and future fadin!
   Fallin!
   Beggin!
   Screamin!

Z. And little lights!
   You tell the moon!
   You tell the planets!

A. There are children bein dropped from the sky and nobody is
   catchin them!

Z. You write this on the sky for all to see!

A. There are children bein dropped from the sky!

Z. This she promises, to never sparkle for anyone again!

A. There are children!

   A *loses her sparkles.*
   Z *vomits up glitter and tears out the sparkles from inside her.*
   It is a painful procedure.

THE THIRD CHAPTER

One

Z. Hey Judgy Eyes came back!
   Go fetch Judgy Eyes their gift.

   A *brings out a huge pair of sunglasses.*

   You are goin to love this gift Judgy Eyes.

A. For you and your judgy eyes! Put them on!

   Hopefully they do?

Z. They love it.

A. They love it.

Z. Brilliant just stay like that forever.

A. On with the story? We get to meet your fella.

Z. He's not my fella.

A. He's so borin. He's like if a shop mannequin tried to pass as
   a human bein.

Z. What about your partner? That's healthy. Not.

A. Me and her are actually really happy so fuck you.
   Let's carry on the story.

Z. In three.

A. Two.

Z. One.

A. Boom.

   Loud thumping music blasts on. The TWINS *begin to dance
   wildly and freely. It becomes a raging roaring
   choreographed dance.*

Two

Thirteen years later. A brings on Mannequin Man and begins to operate him.

Z. I hate you.

> *A staffroom. Z is trapped in a conversation with Mannequin Man.*

A / MANNEQUIN MAN. Hey babe.
So Patsy says we're getting a Waitrose.

Z. Did she?

A / MANNEQUIN MAN. Yeah Patsy says we're getting a Waitrose.

Z. I need to tell you somethin.

A / MANNEQUIN MAN. It was very competitive.

Z. What?

A / MANNEQUIN MAN. Getting the Waitrose.
Patsy says it was very competitive.

Z. Are we still speakin about that?

A / MANNEQUIN MAN. Very competitive.
I really think we've earned it though.
Getting the Waitrose.
I really think we've earned it.
We're good people.

Z. Could I speak –

A / MANNEQUIN MAN. Good people.
Sorry babe, how was the doctor's appointment?
Let me just stop you babe.
Patsy was saying she served a man who looked just like her doctor.

Z. Could I speak –

A / MANNEQUIN MAN. You're confused.
It wasn't actually Patsy's doctor, it just looked like Patsy's doctor.

Z. No I understand, I just don't give a fuck.

A / MANNEQUIN MAN. Let me explain.
It wasn't actually Patsy's doctor, it just –

Z. I'm pregnant.

A / MANNEQUIN MAN. … .

Z. Twins.

A / MANNEQUIN MAN. …

Z. They're yours.
I haven't had disappointin sex with anyone else.

A / MANNEQUIN MAN. I cannot be dealing with this right now.

I'm sorry.
Let's just sit down shall we?

*After some struggle, Mannequin Man sits down. Then he
effortlessly manspreads his legs as wide as they can
possibly go.*

Now are you sure?

Z. Yup.

A / MANNEQUIN MAN. Do you know what the menstrual
cycle is?
Let me explain.
The menstrual cycle starts on the first day of your period
and ends when –

Z. Shut up!

A / MANNEQUIN MAN. How far gone?

Z. Twelve weeks.
I don't know how cuz the sex was shit.

A / MANNEQUIN MAN. You know you can be really
unlikeable sometimes.
Who even are you? It's like you've buried yourself down.
Patsy has you for Secret Santa
and she asks me what you'd like and I have no idea!

Z. Thanks for spoilin it.
I was lookin forward to Patsy's shit present.

A / MANNEQUIN MAN. After that night I told Patsy we had
truly connected.

Z. It was five minutes by a skip.
Wait you told Patsy?

A / MANNEQUIN MAN. I say Patsy
'Girls Just Want to Have Fun' played and she started sobbing
and we truly connected.

I've worked with you for years and I have no idea who
you are!
You always eat alone.
You're cold to customers!
You're even colder to us!
Who are you?
What do you love!?

Z. Not you.

A / MANNEQUIN MAN. Why are you such a bitch?

Sorry.

It's just.

You can be really unlikeable sometimes.

Patsy is scared of you.
Every time you walk past she does a little wee.

Z. Good.

A / MANNEQUIN MAN. I was going to do a PowerPoint
presentation on your uterus for you.
But whatever, I don't think I'll bother now.

Z. See you at the birth.

A / MANNEQUIN MAN. Yeah whatever.
I need to get back on the floor so I'm going to walk away now.

*Mannequin Man walks away. Sort of. As much as a
mannequin can walk away.*

Okay I don't have any legs so I need you to carry me over
there.

*Z carries the Mannequin Man away. She is then left alone.
With all the self-hate in the world, she pulls her hair and
slaps her face. She makes a fist ready to punch herself in the
stomach but can't bring herself to do it. She roars out as pain
leaks from her face.*

Three

A sits by the door howling and whining. She is suffering from separation anxiety.
She scratches at the door and chews the frame. She runs back to her phone on the floor and tries to ring a number again. She chews up cushions and returns to howling by the door.

Human Partner enters and A begins panting and salivating.
She jumps on top of her.

A. *AWOOOOOOOO!!!*
HOOOOMAAAN PARTNER!! I MISSED YOU!

   A licks her face over and over again.

Z / HUMAN PARTNER. Eight missed calls?

A. It was you who got me the howl tube!

Z / HUMAN PARTNER. For emergencies.

   A begins to whine.

A. Are you mad?

Z / HUMAN PARTNER. I'm not mad.

A. Where you goin!? Where you goin!?

Z / HUMAN PARTNER. Kitchen.

A. Wait for me!
I follow! I follow!
Did you bring me meat?

Z / HUMAN PARTNER. No.

A. Are you gonna cook for me?

Z / HUMAN PARTNER. Riley is coming to stay for the weekend remember?

A. Cook for me!

Z / HUMAN PARTNER. You need to stop being scared of the hob.

A. I'm not scared of the burny meat ring!

Z / HUMAN PARTNER. Remember what I said about the bowls!?

A. 'Bein hoooomaaan is leavin bowls to soak.'
  Are you mad?
  I brushed my head fur today like you taught me.

Z / HUMAN PARTNER. Did you look for work?

A. I ate some poop.

Z / HUMAN PARTNER. Did you look for work?

A. I tried to ask
  the hoooomaaan who shoves dead trees through our den for
  his job.

Z / HUMAN PARTNER. Start calling things by their names.

A. But then I was annoyed cuz he was on our territory so
  I bit him.

Z / HUMAN PARTNER. You need to look for work.

A. We can do that together on the weekend.

Z / HUMAN PARTNER. My weekends aren't just for you!
  They're for Riley and stop biting humans!

A. I'm sorry!

Z / HUMAN PARTNER. Right I'm picking him up from his
  dad's. You staying in?

A. Yeah I'm just gonna howl at the moon for a bit.

Z / HUMAN PARTNER. No more howling at the moon, the
  neighbours are complaining!

A. I'm a wolf silly.

Z / HUMAN PARTNER. How would we survive if we get
  thrown out?

A. I'm really good at diggin dens.

Z / HUMAN PARTNER. Sit there and be human.

A. Stay and have a hot river drink?

Z / HUMAN PARTNER. I'll be five minutes tops.

A. Promise me you'll come back!?

Z / HUMAN PARTNER. Five fucking minutes.

A. Could you ask Riley not to spread his scent on you?
I know he's your tiny hairless hoooomaaan pup
but I just find it a little uncomfortable.

Z / HUMAN PARTNER. Did you get his room ready?

A. I forgot! forgot!

Z / HUMAN PARTNER. I'll do it.

> *Human Partner exits. A tries to resist the urge to howl at the moon but gives into the howling.*
> *Human Partner re-enters.*

Hey babe, have you seen Riley's hamster?

A. …

Z / HUMAN PARTNER. His hamster, have you seen it?

A. I ate it.

Z / HUMAN PARTNER. What?

A. Have I done somethin wrong?

Z / HUMAN PARTNER. You ate his hamster!?

A. It was prey.

Z / HUMAN PARTNER. It was his pet hamster!

A. It was tasty.

Z / HUMAN PARTNER. You're insane.

A. Are you mad?

Z / HUMAN PARTNER. YES!

A. I'll buy him a new one.

Z / HUMAN PARTNER. With what money?

A. I'm sorry.

Z / HUMAN PARTNER. This is exhausting.

A. I said we should sleep durin the day! I'm a nocturnal animal!

Z / HUMAN PARTNER. You're exhausting.

A. I don't know what I need to do?

Z / HUMAN PARTNER. Stop pissing all over the house!

A. I'm markin my territory!
   There are a lot of predators eyein up this den.

Z / HUMAN PARTNER. Stop challenging random chihuahuas
   to fight to the death!

A. I didn't like the way you were strokin her!

Z / HUMAN PARTNER. Be human!

A. I'm tryin to be hoooomaaan!

Z / HUMAN PARTNER. Try harder!

A. You make everythin seem so effortless.
   When I'm next to you I feel like a firefly tryin to shine as
   bright as the sun.
   But you gotta know every single day I am tryin.

Z / HUMAN PARTNER. I'm sorry you never got a normal
   childhood but you need to stop this!

A. I'm sorry!

Z / HUMAN PARTNER. You need to get over it!
   That's what I say to my huge family and massive support
   system of friends.
   She needs to get over it!

A. Be patient.
   You're patient with light at night cuz you know it will
   come back
   yet you're not patient with me!

Z / HUMAN PARTNER. Because I want a human relationship!
   You know Riley hates the way you eat.
   He asks if he can eat in his room because you make him
   feel sick!

A. I'm no good with hoooomaaan words but I know I have love
   to give.
   I can feel the sparkles and glitter buzzin around my head.
   I could give it to you?

   A *begins to sparkle and breathe out tiny bits of glitter.*

   For you.
   It's all for you.

Z / HUMAN PARTNER. ...

A. Love me?

Z / HUMAN PARTNER. I remember when I first heard your wild heart
beating out of time with every other human.

I thought it was the most beautiful sound I had ever heard

and I wanted to hear it every day of my life.

My wild girl.

But I need more than that wild beat.

I deserve more than that wild beat.

A. I licked your face and you didn't get angry.

You just smiled.

Z / HUMAN PARTNER. You did a really good job of brushing your hair.

A. I did!?

Z / HUMAN PARTNER. It looks really nice.

I want you out of here by tomorrow morning.

Four

Strontium's house. She sits wearing her red jumper and a headscarf, looking tired and weak. Z stands.

A / STRONTIUM. You don't need to stay Francium...

Z. I can make you some food Strontium?

A / STRONTIUM. Everything tastes like metal.

Z. Have you tried eatin metal? Maybe that tastes like –

A / STRONTIUM. It still tastes like metal.

Z. Let me make you some food?

A / STRONTIUM. You can't cook.

Z. I can cook!

A / STRONTIUM. You can burn.

Z. You ate my burn before.

A / STRONTIUM. Barely.

Z. It's all comin out now.

A / STRONTIUM. Dying does that.

Z. Don't say that.

Have you heard we're gettin a Waitrose?

A / STRONTIUM. When?

Z. Next year.

A / STRONTIUM. Oh.

Strontium starts removing her headscarf. Z can't look.
Strontium does it back up again.

Z. So the Waitrose is somethin to look forward to, isn't it?

A / STRONTIUM. Francium will you sit the fuck down?

Z. Okay sittin the fuck down.

Z sits down. There are loads of university prospectuses on
the chair. She picks them up and groans.

A / STRONTIUM. Best universities for chemistry in the
country!

Z. It's becomin obsessive.

A / STRONTIUM. You look as scared as when I threw you that
surprise sixteenth party.
Spent the whole night in the cupboard.

Z. I liked that cupboard.
You had to threaten everyone with a detention so they
would come.

She wouldn't come.

A moment.

A / STRONTIUM. How is

she?

Z. I'm pregnant.

A / STRONTIUM. But it was five minutes by a skip?

A moment.

Are you

keeping.

Z. I think so?

Twins.

I'm sorry Strontium.

A / STRONTIUM. Why on earth are you sorry Francium?

Z. You're disappointed.

A / STRONTIUM. Never.

Wow you're going to be a mum.

Z. There are so many people who want this more than me.

Who pay for this.

Who beg for this.

Who deserve this.

And then to me

it just happens.

A / STRONTIUM. You're going to be a great mum.
Just never cook for them.

Z. Please let me make you some food?

A / STRONTIUM. I plan to die from cancer, not food
poisoning.

I'm going to try and stick around to meet them Francium.

My God I'm going to try.

Now have you told your mum?

Five

A sits behaving feral on a night bus.
She opens up the window and feels the night air on her face.
She watches the world pass her by.

A. You sit on the night bus.
  Feel it buzz and shake and move and hum.
  Everyone gets off the night bus and goes back to their dens.
  But you got no den to go back to so you sit on the night bus
  all night long.

  So you sleep on the night bus.
  Feel the holes in the yawnin road rock you to sleep.
  Smell its damp and piss in your dreams.

Z / WOODPECKER. The Woodpecker has arrived!
  Peck. Peck. Peck.
  Sorry I haven't checked up on you in years hoooomaaan.
  I cannot stay long as I saw a tasty worm outside.

A. I'm really sad Woodpecker.

Z / WOODPECKER. Hoooomaaan it is polite to offer a bird
  bath for flying visitors.

A. I feel like I never stopped fallin from that day you dropped me.

Z / WOODPECKER. You're just not trying hard enough to
  integrate hoooomaaan.
  You should be driving this bus not sleeping on it.

A. Woodpecker I feel so alone.

Z / WOODPECKER. I couldn't relate.
  I have so many friends.

A. I'm findin it really hard Woodpecker.

Z / WOODPECKER. You have your freedom. Peck. Peck. Peck.

A. This ain't freedom.
  It's loneliness.
  You wouldn't treat your own children like this
  so why treat me in this way?
  I want to start again.
  Sometimes Woodpecker, I imagine tearin off my skin and
  startin again and –

  Woodpecker's mobile phone rings. Woodpecker answers it.

Z / WOODPECKER. Hey son!
    No I'm not busy!
    Are you okay?
    Sorry to hear that love.
    You know I always thought her mating dance was shit.
    You can do better.
    Who's keeping the nest?
    What a bitch. I'll peck her fucking eyes out.
    You can stay with me for as long as you need.
    You'll always have a home here.
    I'll get some of your favourite nuts in.
    Yeah Marks and Spencer.
    Speak to you soon.
    I love you.
    I love you.
    I love you.

A. Does Ma mention me?

Z / WOODPECKER. Speaking about the furry parent will not
    help during this transitional period.
    Peck. Peck. Peck.

A. She believed in me so it made me believe in me.
    But it's gettin so much harder to believe in me Woodpecker.

Z / WOODPECKER. She has taken in a new hoooomaaan.

A. ...

Z / WOODPECKER. She feeds him.
    She licks him.
    She cuddles him.
    And his smile is so big on his tiny face
    that we the birds can see it from the sky.

    Well this is my stop.

A. Will you stay?
    Will you stay a little longer?
    Cuz I'd like to get to know you?
    And maybe you'd like to get to know me?

Z / WOODPECKER. The check-up is complete.
    You just have to integrate more.
    Independent hoooomaaan living! Peck. Peck. Peck.

You know you were one of the lucky ones.
You had a kind furry parent.
I know a hoooomaaan who was raised by butterflies
and they only fed her sweat and tears through her feet.
So quit your bitching!

Woodpecker flies away.

A. We should all be the lucky ones.

Six

A waiting room.
Shit waiting-room music plays.

A / INSANE MUM. Mmm.

Z. What?

A / INSANE MUM. I didn't say anything.

Z. ...

   A moment.

A / INSANE MUM. Is your scan after mine?

Z. Yeah.

   A moment.

A / INSANE MUM. Is this your *first*?

Z. Yeah.

A / INSANE MUM. *Only* your *first*?

Z. Yeah.

A / INSANE MUM. Make sure you take a selfie with the
   afterbirth.
   This is my *fourth*.

Z. I'm havin twins.

A / INSANE MUM. I'm having *triplets*.
   What trimester are you in?

Z. Second.

A / INSANE MUM. *Only* your *second*?
I'm in my *third*.

Of course it's not a competition
If it was I would win.

They would give me a little gold cup because I would win.

But it's not a competition.

But if it was

they would give me a little gold cup because I would win.

Is your partner not with you?

Z. We're not together.

A / INSANE MUM. Oh my.

Who decorated your uterus?
Laurence Llewelyn-Bowen decorated mine.

Z. No one.

A / INSANE MUM. Have you chosen a retirement home for
your twins yet?
Places fill up fast.
Have you started shitting out sparkles for them yet?
I shat sparkles for months.
Would you like to see a photo of my youngest?

She brings one out.

Z. I'm fine.

A / INSANE MUM. Look at it.
Form an opinion.
Isn't he perfect?
You can keep that photo.

Z. I don't want.

A / INSANE MUM. KEEP IT.

He did a poo in the shape of a heart today.
I mean I had to make it into a heart myself but it was
still adorable.
I have it with me, would you like to see it?

Z. NO.

A / INSANE MUM. My breast milk tastes like champagne.
Would you like to try it?

Z. NO.

A / INSANE MUM. So it's agreed your twins are going to
marry my triplets?
Perhaps my third triplet could marry your afterbirth?
Let's set a date for the wedding?

Z. I need to go.

A / INSANE MUM. How is next summer for you?
Would you like to see my middle child's baby teeth?

Z. No thank you.

Insane Mum brings out a bag of her child's teeth.

A / INSANE MUM. I'll make you up a bag to take home.
Would you like to sniff my child's baby teeth?

Z. What?

Insane Mum brings out a mirror.
She begins to crush up the teeth.
She uses a credit card to sweep the powder into lines.
She rolls up a note begins to snort the teeth powder from the
mirror.
Z watches in disbelief.

A / INSANE MUM. FUCK YEAH! FUCK YEAH! FUCK
YEAH!
I FUCKING LOVE BEING A MUM
I'm sorry, would you like to sniff them?

Z. I'm not ready for this.
I can't do this.

Seven

A food bank. Z begins stacking up tins. With each new tin placed on the ground, A feels her dignity torn away.

A. I don't want them to see this bit.

Z. We need to tell it.

A. I feel so low it's like the underground is above me.

Z. You've done nothin wrong by bein here.

A. I'm so hungry.

Z. Judgy Eyes put your glasses back on.

A. That forever feelin in your bones.
It sinks on down down down to your tummy.

And the hoooomaaans won't let me hunt squirrels or foxes or dogs.
But them same hoooomaaans won't give me food so I come here.

And I think about the clever hoooomaaans who find it so easy to just buy food.

They can just buy food.

I arrive at 8:10 and there are already fifty-four of us waitin.
I try to keep on countin to make the forever feelin in my tummy go away.

Sixty

Seventy

Eighty

Until it gets past numbers I can count.

And in this line
there is a child raised by slugs who is scared of salt.
A child raised by bats who is scared of light.
A child raised by dung beetles who can't get that smell out.
We were all made to stand on our two legs but never taught how.

And I go in.

Metal stones of food to keep us alive.
And it's like I can hear all the metal stones laughin at me.

There's a little lady and she smiles and I think that smile
saves my life.
The little lady asks me for my red voucher and I'm so
embarrassed to get it out.
But I do cuz I have to eat.
She gives me metal stones of meat
and them things I need for when I paint the ground red.

She tells me it's okay.

She touches my arm.

She treats me like I'm hoooomaaan.

The little lady asks if I want some food.
I don't wanna eat in front of her
cuz I know it makes hoooomaaans uncomfortable.

But I gotta eat
and she's gotta watch me eat.
And as I eat
and as she's watchin me eat
I try to tell her how sorry I am that she has to watch
somethin
as disgustin as me eat.

Z. Let's make the tins speak.

A. Nah.

Z. Why?

A. Cuz we'll still be here.
And we'll still need these places.
And talkin tins won't make that go away.

I see a woman and she has her little boy with her.

And he's eatin quicker than I have ever seen any
hoooomaaan eat before.

And she's just starin
like she's starin at the most beautiful thing she has ever seen.

Like in this moment all is right in this broken world.

Eight

Z is getting her second ultrasound scan.

Z. Fuck me! That's cold!

A / SONOGRAPHER. Sorry. Is this your first pregnancy?

Z. Yup. Is this your first scan?

A / SONOGRAPHER. Couple of hundred love.

Z. Seen many ugly foetuses today?

A / SONOGRAPHER. First-time pregnancy and having twins? You're brave.

Z. No, I'm really not.

A / SONOGRAPHER. How are you feeling?

Z. Sleepy. Crampy. Vaginal dischargey –

A / SONOGRAPHER. All perfectly normal.

Z. And I'm always really horny –

A / SONOGRAPHER. Let's start.

Z. Do you get bored of lookin at foetuses all day?

A / SONOGRAPHER. Please let's start.

Z. Not even a tiny bit bored?

A / SONOGRAPHER. No I quite enjoy it.

Z. I guess you have to. Like there's nothin else you can do now is there?

A moment.

A / SONOGRAPHER. I'd like to have been a Meat Loaf impersonator.

Okay are you ready?

*Z looks across the stage and sees the Soggy Woman.
It haunts her.*

Z. What was your mum like? It's just you seem well adjusted?

A / SONOGRAPHER. …

Z. Sorry too personal.
I've crossed the sacred ultrasound line.

A / SONOGRAPHER. It's fine – I mean you actually have
crossed the sacred ultrasound line...

Z. ...

A / SONOGRAPHER. ...

Z. What if my soul sinks in shallow waters like hers did?

A / SONOGRAPHER. Why don't you ask them yourself?
You're having two baby girls.

Z. What?

*Her unborn babies appear in the form of two foetus puppets
with giant eyes.
They are floating in the womb having the time of their lives.
Fuckloads of movement.*

A / FOETUS 1. HEY MA!

A / FOETUS 2. HEY MA!

A / FOETUS 1. WATCH ME MOVE MY ARM MA!

A / FOETUS 2. WATCH ME MOVE MY LEG MA!

Z. HEYYYYY LITTLE ONES!

A / FOETUS 1. Why are you speakin to us in that voice?
It's a little bit offensive.

Z. I'm sorry. It's just the voice you speak to babies in.

A / FOETUS 1. It's a little bit offensive.

A / FOETUS 2. WATCH ME MOVE MY LEG MA!

Z. Wow.

A / FOETUS 1. WATCH ME MOVE MY ARM MA!

Z. I'm watchin your sister at the moment.

A / FOETUS 1. WATCH ME MA!

Z. How do I make them stop?

A / FOETUS 1. We've been readin in the womb library.

A / FOETUS 2. About the outside.

A / FOETUS 1. We're a little apprehensive.

A / FOETUS 2. What if we stop breathin?

A / FOETUS 1. What if you let us cry too much?

A / FOETUS 2. What if you drop us on our heads?

A / FOETUS 1. What if we don't learn to talk?

A / FOETUS 2. What if we don't make friends on the first day of school?

A / FOETUS 1. What if we get shit roles in the Nativity?

A / FOETUS 2. What if the earth spins so fast and we fall off?

Z. I will never let you fall.

She cuddles them tight but dreads them speaking again.

A / FOETUS 2. What if the sun explodes?

A / FOETUS 1. And the oceans rise?

A / FOETUS 2. And the ice caps melt?

A / FOETUS 1. THE ICE CAPS ARE MELTIN.

A / FOETUS 2. THE ICE CAPS ARE MELTIN.

Z. I'll stop them.

A / FOETUS 1. What if you get sad like she did and shrivel in the bath?

Z. No.

A / FOETUS 2. Swallow the light from our world?

Z. Please stop?

A / FOETUS 1. What if you don't love us?

A / FOETUS 2. What if you can't love us?

A / FOETUS 1. Because if you weren't loved as a child how can you possibly love us?

Z. STOP! Turn it off!

A / SONOGRAPHER. But.

Z. TURN IT OFF!

Her unborn babies disappear.

A / SONOGRAPHER. Would you like a scan photo?

Z. FUCK OFF MEAT LOAF!

Nine

A Jobcentre office. A behaves feral throughout.

Z / BRENDA. Customer number four hundred and twenty-two.
I'm Brenda.
Are you here today to sign on you piece of shit?

A. Yes…

Z / BRENDA. Okay you scrounger.
You need to speak to Brenda on floor two.
Up the stairs on your left.

A. Thanks.

Z / BRENDA. I hope you die on the way there.

Z / BRENDA. Customer number one thousand and five.
I'm Brenda.
I was voted most likely to have ate my twin in the womb.
Are you here today to sign on you cunt?

A. Yes.

Z / BRENDA. Okay.

Hello.

A. Hello.

Z / BRENDA. That was not a satisfactory answer.
I'm going to have to stop your benefits.
You have five seconds to appeal this decision.
If you wish to appeal you can speak to Brenda on floor seven.
Off you fuck now.

Z / BRENDA. Customer number one million and sixty-two.
I'm Brenda.
I feed KFC to chickens because it makes me feel like a god.
Are you here to repeal a sanctioning?

I'm just going to ask you a few questions
and then we will reconsider the decision.

She brings out a huge image of a blobfish.

Look at the image of a blobfish.
Study the image of a blobfish.
Tell me why this blobfish is so sad?

A. I don't know.

Z / BRENDA. WHY IS THIS BLOBFISH SO SAD!?

Okay and that's all the information we need today.
We'll let you know the outcome very soon.
And it's a no.
In the meantime if you're struggling with your life
I can refer you to a hard-times charity.

Z / BRENDA. Customer number fifty million and twenty-one.
I'm Brenda.
I think having postcards of spiritual quotes makes me a good
person.

I'm here to help you.

No

Not help.

Save.

I'm here to save you.

A. Can I –

Z / BRENDA. I just want to say.
What you have been through is so inspiring.

A. I don't want to be inspirin.
I want to be happy.

Z / BRENDA. You've been through hell and you don't let it get
you down.

A. I'm really sad.

Z / BRENDA. And I'm here to listen to *you*.

Okay let me just put this muzzle on you so you can't speak.

For you to access my charity resources I'll need a next of kin.
Do you know what a next of kin is?
For example if you're injured who would we ring?

A. I don't know.

Z / BRENDA. It's okay. It's okay.
If you died who would care?

A. I don't know!

Z / BRENDA. Would anyone care if you died?

A. I don't know!

Z / BRENDA. It's okay. It's okay.

A. I'm sorry.

Z / BRENDA. Let's just write no one shall we?

NO ONE.
Now how can I help?

A. I need –

Z / BRENDA. Because I love saving people.
I push small children down wells just so I can save them.

A. Food?

Z / BRENDA. The other day I saw this woman with
horrendous hair.
I mean not as horrendous as yours but still horrendous.

A. A den?

Z / BRENDA. I cut off my hair and glued it to her head.

A. A pack?

Z / BRENDA. I gave my kidney to a boy.

A. Help me?

Z / BRENDA. This little boy falls and grazes his knee.

A. Help me?

Z / BRENDA. Everyone starts panicking but Brenda thinks fast.

A. HELP ME!!!

Z / BRENDA. I cut out my kidney and hand it to him.

A. HELP ME!!!!!!!!!!!

Z / BRENDA. I say Take It.
TAKE MY KIDNEY
I stuff it in his pocket and just walk away.

A. I NEED HELP!!!

Z / BRENDA. Just walk away.

   A *tears off the muzzle*.

A. Help me!

   I need someone to listen!

   I need to be asked how I am!

   I need to know someone cares!

Z / BRENDA. Do you need my kidney?

A. I need to know I matter!
Show me that I matter!

Z / BRENDA. Do you need my kidney?

A. I don't need your kidney!

Z / BRENDA. You need my kidney.
I'm going to save you.

   *Brenda grabs a clicky pen and stabs herself in the abdomen.
   She slowly pulls out her kidney from her body, blood, guts
   and absurdity spill out on the floor.
   Brenda tries to hand her kidney to A.*

   TAKE MY KIDNEY.

A. Will you listen!?

Z / BRENDA. TAKE MY FUCKING KIDNEY.

   Brenda passes out probably dead.

A. Help?

   Help?

   A *whimpers*.

Ten

Z is playing Monopoly with Strontium.

Z. 'Go to jail. Do not pass Go. Do not collect two hundred pounds.'

Strontium smashes up the Monopoly board.

Sore loser.

A / STRONTIUM. I'm stopping chemo.

Z. You're givin up.

A / STRONTIUM. It isn't giving up.

Z. Well it isn't fightin.

A / STRONTIUM. I'm listening to what I have left of my body.

Z. You said you would stick around.
One more round?

A moment.

A / STRONTIUM. I wanted to meet them so badly Francium.

You give your entire life to chemical composition and it fucks you up the arse.
I was never good at science anyway.

Z. I need to go.
Lots to do.

A / STRONTIUM. Why are you pretending you have a life all of a sudden Francium?

Z. Don't call me that.

A / STRONTIUM. You don't have a life Francium.

Z. Lots to do.

A / STRONTIUM. For years you've given up.

Z. ...

A / STRONTIUM. You barely exist.
You barely fight.
You barely breathe.

Z. ...

A / STRONTIUM. And you say I've given up!?
I see you taking as shallow breaths as possible.
Standing in the shade so you don't have a shadow.
Afraid to laugh, live or love.
I haven't seen you smile in years Francium.

Z. …

A / STRONTIUM. If I was good at science want to know what
I would do?

I would shrink myself down.
I would climb up your nose into your brain and beg this pain
to stop.

If I was good at science I would build a time machine
to see that girl who used to explode with ideas and wonder
for this world.

I miss your laugh.
I wish you would laugh more.

And I wish you'd fight, even just a tiny bit.
Because you're so young and you might not think you are
but you are so young.
I have done my years of fighting but you've not even begun.
And those little ones are going to need someone who can
fight.

And I wish I could take that pain away
but I can't.
So what use is science?

If I can't see you smile?

If I can't see you laugh?

If I can't see you fight?

What use is science?

Z. …

A / STRONTIUM. If you say it, I'll say it back.

I promise I'll say it back.

Z. I need to go.

A / STRONTIUM. I love you.

Z. ...

A / STRONTIUM. Like you were mine.

 Like you came from me.

 Like you're a part of me.

 I fucking love you Francium.

 Please stay?

Z. Another game?

Strontium makes up the board. Her arm sparkles.
Z stares in wonder like she's waited her entire life for this
moment.

Eleven

A *is in her first job interview. She sits panting.*
Butcher goes to give A *a handshake.* A *looks confused and tilts*
her head. She licks Butcher's face.

A. You need to lick me back silly.
 You're like an old grumpy tree.

Z / BUTCHER. Let's begin.
 This isn't just a butcher's. This is a Waitrose butcher.

 I don't know what that means.
 I just got told to say it.

 I'm going to ask you some questions.

 Tell me what you know about Waitrose?

A. Green light.

Z / BUTCHER. Good enough for me.

A. Do you wanna sniff my bum?

Z / BUTCHER. No.
 Tell me about a time you were able to prioritise duties and
 think on your feet?

A. I drunk out of a toilet bowl this mornin cuz I was thirsty.

Z / BUTCHER. Tell me about a time you had to multitask?

A. Well Butcher Man,
this one time I rolled in somethin wet then I rolled in somethin smelly.

I should have done it the other way around.

Z / BUTCHER. I see.

A. How am I doin?
I think I would make a brilliant butcher! I love meat!

Z / BUTCHER. Well thanks for coming in.
We'll be letting candidates know in a few days' time.

A. I know this is just a job to you but to me this is everythin.

I might not speak the right hoooomaaan words but I can do this.
I know I can do this yo.

I'm askin for you to catch me.

Please please catch me?

Cuz I need to be caught so bad.

Z / BUTCHER. Thanks for coming in.

A. Okay.

I like your hoooomaaan hat.

A *sadly nears the exit. She begins to examine the butcher table.*

Are you throwin this away?

Z / BUTCHER. Yup.
No one will buy it.

A. Silly hoooomaaan, everyone would buy this if they knew about it.

Z / BUTCHER. Would they now?

A. Are you throwin this part away as well!?

Z / BUTCHER. Yup.

A. Wow you really don't know anythin about meat do you?
   You could sell this.

Z / BUTCHER. Could I now?

A. You hoooomaaans are so stoopid Butcher Man.
   I'm an expert mate.
   When me and Ma would hunt I would always go for this part!
   Over the belly, right next to the spare ribs!
   It's the most sneakiest most tasty, most-mostest part ever!

Z / BUTCHER. You really like meat don't you?

A. I really love meat Butcher Man

Z / BUTCHER. You start on Monday.

Twelve

Strontium's red jumper is attached to obvious strings and begins to float away.

Z. Will you stay!?
   Will you stay a little longer!?

   The red jumper waves goodbye.

   There were things I was goin to say.

   The red jumper waves goodbye again.
   Z tries to hold on to it.

   Z realises there is nothing else she can do now but wave goodbye.
   The red jumper floats away.

   Some moments pass.

   Her unborn babies appear.

A / FOETUS 1. HEY MA!

A / FOETUS 2. HEY MA!

Z. Now isn't the best time.

A / FOETUS 1. CAN YOU FEEL ME MOVE MY ARM MA! ?

A / FOETUS 2. CAN YOU FEEL ME MOVE MY LEG MA!?

Z. Please fuck off.

Her unborn babies sing a bit to try and cheer her up.

Very nice.

A / FOETUS 1. Thanks Ma.
Your liver runs a record label
We're feelin pretty confident it's goin to sign us.

Z. ...

A / FOETUS 1. You feel sad Ma?
Have you heard we're gettin a Waitrose!?

Z. I am sad.

A / FOETUS 2. Who was she Ma?

Z. She was the woman who raised me and I miss her.

A / FOETUS 1. Don't be sad Ma.

Z. I can't help it.

A / FOETUS 2. That's it we're comin out for cuddles!

Z. You're not ready. I'm not ready.

A / FOETUS 1. We just can't wait to meet you Ma!
We've been readin in the womb library about cuddles.
We've become cuddle connoisseurs!

Z. You'll never get to meet her.
She'll just be a photograph to you.

A / FOETUS 1. We would have loved her like you did.

A / FOETUS 2. Ma sometimes at night we watch the neurons in
your brain.

A / FOETUS 1. We know it's a restricted area.

A / FOETUS 2. But we love lookin at them.

A / FOETUS 1. All those dreams buzzin around you.

A / FOETUS 2. We see your heart and it is a beautiful heart.
We see the holes where the sparkles should be.

A / FOETUS 1. We feel how you don't expect it to beat any more because it's broken.
But it carries on pumpin beat after beat after beat.

A / FOETUS 2. Sometimes we just listen to it beat all night.

A / FOETUS 1. We're not expectin you to be perfect.

A / FOETUS 2. Sometimes we'll be right dickheads and cry fuckloads.

A / FOETUS 1. And maybe everyone will forget your identity after you become a mum.
And then you'll feel like you're losin yourself all over again.

A / FOETUS 2. But know that when we gaze into your eyes.

A / FOETUS 1. We are tellin you we love you.

A / FOETUS 2. We are tellin you when the ice caps melt.

A / FOETUS 1. We wanna be right next to you.

A / FOETUS 2. Don't cry Ma!
Look at what you did sis!

Z. What if this world breaks you?
What if I break you!?

A / FOETUS 1. That's it we're comin out!

Z. Don't you dare come out of my vagina!

A / FOETUS 1. You need a cuddle and we are cuddle connoisseurs!

Z. I'm not ready! I'm not ready! I'm not ready!

Her waters break. There is a flood. Things break. She is scared.

Thirteen

A *is attempting to chop up meat with a butcher knife. She gives up and goes back to biting the meat.*

A. *GRRRRRRRRR!!!*

Z / BUTCHER. Use the knife. It took me time to learn as well.

A. IT'S HARD!

Z / BUTCHER. Let's not fall out. You did a really good job today.

Use the knife.

A *attempts to use the knife again and gives up again.*

Use the knife.

A. Stoopid hoooomaaan and his stooopid hat!

Z / BUTCHER. I thought you liked my hat.
Use the knife.

A *attempts to use the knife again.*

Take away that heavier piece of fat.
Long strips.
Don't saw.
Don't hack!
Use the entire knife.
Straight strips.

Be careful you're gonna cut your finger off.

A. I don't care.

Z / BUTCHER. You're gonna cut your finger off!

A. I don't care!
FUCK.
GRRRRRRRRRRRRRRR!

A *begins to bleed from her finger.*

Z / BUTCHER. And you've cut your finger off.

Show me.

Shit.

Put a plaster on it then.

A. The way you look at me sometimes.

Z / BUTCHER. Put a plaster on it.

A. Like I'm dumb.
Like I'm filthy.
Like I'm stooopid.

Z / BUTCHER. Fine bleed to death.

A. Cuz I'm not.

Z / BUTCHER. I never said you were.

A. Your eyes does.

Z / BUTCHER. No they don't.

A. Your eyes Butcher Man
At lunchtime.
The way I eat.
The way I look.
The way I stand.

Z / BUTCHER. Please go put a plaster on.

A. It's okay for you.
With your family holidays.
And your herbs.
And your Waitrose.

Z / BUTCHER. That's enough.

A. And your ugly kids!
And their ugly happy childhood!
And your ugly house!
With its ugly roof!
And your ugly parents!
And your ugly siblins!
And your ugly happy life!
And your ugly Christmases and birthdays!
And your ugly next of kin!
And your ugly safety blanket!
And your ugly existence!
But what about me!?

Z / BUTCHER. I WAS A CHILD OF THE WOODS TOO!

A. ...

Z / BUTCHER. You think a normal hoooomaaan would have hired you?

I was raised by the trees.

A. That's why you're so grumpy.

Z / BUTCHER. I'm not grumpy.
I'm chilled.

A. Why didn't you say?

Z / BUTCHER. Because maybe after all these years I'm still ashamed?

Edna was her name. She probably doesn't even remember me.

I saw in you the same fear I had.
I felt that forever feeling in your bones.

I remember my boy's sixteenth birthday.
He wanted to go out with his mates and I wouldn't let him.
I was so desperate to make it clear
he could stay with us for as long as he wanted.
This would always be his home.
No Woodpecker would ever come for him.

I remember falling from the sky.

I remember the first time I was jealous of someone else's mum.
He was a child in a supermarket.

A. I remember fallin from the sky.

Z / BUTCHER. I remember feeling like I was disappearing.

A. I remember feelin like I was disappearin.

Z / BUTCHER. I remember the Woodpecker wouldn't look me in the eyes.

A. I remember at first feelin everythin but later feelin nothin.

Z / BUTCHER. I remember being told I was one of the lucky ones.

A. I remember sittin in the library googlin the quickest way to kill myself.

Z / BUTCHER. I remember

my son's first Christmas.

A. I remember

the smiles from strangers.

Z / BUTCHER. I remember

learning to love again and how terrifying that was.

I remember

the way the little lights danced in the night sky.

Like they were saying we've loved for millions of years.

You're only just starting.

A. Do the feelins go away?

Z / BUTCHER. No but you get new ones.

Feelings you never thought you would feel again.

Butcher puts a plaster on A's *finger.*

Let's try again shall we?

Let's always try again.

Fourteen

Z's newborn babies are in an incubator. A *brings on Mannequin Man.*

A / MANNEQUIN MAN. Hey babe. I got you a coffee.

Z. Thanks.

A / MANNEQUIN MAN. But then I remembered I didn't have any hands so I had to leave it there.

Z. They're so tiny.

A / MANNEQUIN MAN. Sorry I was late.
I've been shitting sparkles non-stop.
One moment.

Mannequin Man grunts and shits out sparkles on the floor.

A nurse will come and clean that up.

Z. I can't hold them.
Maybe it's for the best?

A / MANNEQUIN MAN. Have you slept?

Z. I was meant to create lungs which could breathe.
If I can't even do that how am I goin to do anythin?

A / MANNEQUIN MAN. You did an amazing job babe.
They have my eyes.

Z. They're so tiny.

A / MANNEQUIN MAN. They have my eyes.
The doctor said the co-bedding was helping them.
Did she explain to you what co-bedding was? It's urban
slang for –

Z. I know what it is.

A / MANNEQUIN MAN. I'm going back to the café to see if
I can borrow a hand to get you some coffee.
It's a hospital!
There's bound to be a spare hand somewhere!

They are going to be okay right?

I think every bit of me would break if they weren't okay.

Mannequin Man walks away. Sort of. Z speaks to her babies.

Z. Will you stay?
Will you stay a little longer?
Cuz I'd like to get to know you
And maybe you'd like to get to know me?

I'm sorry I failed your lungs.

I'm sorry I couldn't protect you.

I'm sorry the first thing you felt in this world was pain.

But right now I need you to breathe.

Cuz when the sun explodes and the oceans rise and the ice
caps melt
I need you right next to me.

You see a kindness in me which I haven't seen in myself
in years.

You see a heart which could sparkle.

You make me feel like
we could push back all the gravity in this world
and float into space.

Little lights in the sky, please let them grow like seeds in
the sun.
And little lights, I'm goin to need my sparkle back please.

*The sound of a million lights resetting is heard. Z begins to
sparkle for her babies and looks at her sparkle in awe.*

The babies begin to float into the air from happiness.

A / BABY 1. Weeeeeeeeeeee!!

A / BABY 2. Weeeeeeeeeeee!!

Z. Come on down at once!

A / BABY 1. Come float with us Ma! Don't you feel the same?

*Z stands still on the ground wishing she would allow herself
to float.*

Z. Ah fuck it.

Z finally allows herself to float. Floating higher and higher.

*Fuckloads of movement. They float into space. Z watches as
her babies dodge comets and hug planets. She sees all the
stars in the night sky.*

We should go home now.
Our heads might explode or somethin?

A / BABY 1. WAIT! Little lights in the sky! You tell the moon!
You tell the planets!

A / BABY 2. You write this on the sky for all to see!

A / BABY 1. That our ma sparkles for us!

A / BABY 2. That our ma sparkles for us!

Z. That their ma sparkles for them.

They sparkle brighter than the stars.
Maybe everyone shoots glitter guns at them?
Z looks down back to earth and quickly glances at the Soggy
Woman. She feels a sense of guilt.

There's someone I want you to meet.

Fifteen

A struggles to cut the meat with a butcher knife. She roars and
howls out.
She takes a moment to regain herself.

A. New feelins will come.
   Not today but new feelins will come.

   A picks up the knife and returns to cutting. She successfully
   cuts the meat.

Sixteen

Z takes a moment to look at the Soggy Woman for the first time
in a long time.
It's like she sees her as a human being for the first ever time.

Z. My Soggy Woman in the bath.
   Wet and wrinkly in the bath.
   Beauty evaporated in the bath.

   Hi Mum.
   It's me.

   Would you like to meet your grandchildren?

   They're just parkin the car.
   They're six weeks old and already drivin.
   Were we ever that fearless?

   Can you hear me Mum?

A / SOGGY WOMAN. I'm here.

Z. Mum?

It's me.

A / SOGGY WOMAN. I'm here.

Z. I just want to be your daughter in any way I can.

A / SOGGY WOMAN. Soon you'll forget me.
You don't need to love me.
Just don't forget me.

Z. And maybe this is all we'll ever have.
Me beggin you to stay afloat on the bubbles.

A / SOGGY WOMAN. You won't remember how
when you were placed in my arms for the first time
my heart beat quicker than I ever knew it could.

Z. But we can build machines which can breathe air into the
breathless.
For I have seen them be used on my daughters.

A / SOGGY WOMAN. You won't remember how
I would beg the little lights
For strength to move my arms to hug you.

Z. And if we can do that then we can do anythin.

A / SOGGY WOMAN. You won't remember how
you would tell me wonders about this universe.
Wonders taught to you by another mother.
Wonders which I would never get to share.

Z. Everyone should have someone who sparkles for them.

A / SOGGY WOMAN. You won't remember how
my heart would break with each new wonder you learned.

There is no greater agony seeing another woman raise
your child.
Doing so effortlessly what you struggle with.

If I could grant you one thing in this life it would be

may you never know that pain.

Please

may you never know that pain.

Z. Mum.

Strontium once told me that love is the most powerful force on earth.

Stronger than chlorine trifluoride or batrachotoxin.

Because it's Glitter
Rage
Magic
Fire
and Chaos.

And we'll never understand it.

It just is.

Seventeen

A. I need a shit so I think we should stop.

Z. Agreed.

A. No need to tell the rest.

Z. Totally agreed.

A. Don't end on a downer.

Z. No one wants that.

A. Skip the shittest bit.

Z. Go home.

A. Yeah so everyone just fuck off.

Z. Do one Judgy Eyes.

A. Shit they're still here? Why are you still here?

Z. Maybe we should just finish the story?

A. You go first.

Z. You go first.

A. Together?

Z. Together.

There's a Waitrose openin today and the little ones are so excited.

A. Unload the meat.

Z. Okay their dad is excited. He gets to see them on weekends.

A. Store the meat.

Z. Accordin to him today is a big day for the baby books.

A. Cut the meat.

Z. Our first day out.

A. By the time we would have opened we would have already worked for five hours.

Z. Like proper day out. Space didn't count.

A. But I don't mind cuz I love it.

Z. There are so many people here.

A. Butcher Man says I just need to believe that I can do it.

Z. So many people.

A. Cuz he believes I can do it.
   He makes me feel like I could push back all the gravity.

Z. And we humans stand on concreted roots.

A. Makes me feel warmer than I felt in a long time.

Z. Pantin.

A. Like I'm standin next to fire.
   He hands me the sharpy sharp stick to slice the the meat.

Z. And they cut a ribbon and everyone loses their shit.

A. And my paw starts to shake
   but he gently just squeezes my paw and says I got this.
   There's nothin like bein believed in is there?
   It's the only real magic we have in this world.

Z. The Waitrose is open!

A. The Waitrose is open!

Z. We pile in.

A. I'm a tiny bit scared.

Z. It has that new smell.

A. Cut the meat.

Z. Full of possibility.

A. Sell the meat.

Z. Even the canned goods look proud to be there.

A. Cut the meat.

Z. Check out the vegetables.

A. Sell the meat.

Z. But the girls start to get scared so we don't look long.

A. Cut the meat. Sell the meat.

Z. Check out the cheese. It's just fuckin cheese.

A. Cut the meat. Sell the meat.

Z. Check out the meat.

> *The* TWINS *catch each other's eyes The world stops spinning. This lasts for a while.*
> *Neither is sure what the other will do next.*

A. Can I help you with somethin?

Z. Oh no I'm just lookin.

A. Well let me know if you need anythin.
Have a great day.

I like to think I would have known my sister's eyes anywhere.
But in that moment your eyes were just another pair of eyes.

Z. And you said it like you really meant it.
Like you hoped with every bit of your soul that I had
a great day.

Maybe that's what life is about?
Tiny acts of heartbreak mixed with tiny acts of kindness.

A. I wish I said you are my sister.

Z. You are my sister.

A. You are my sister.
   Could we begin again?
   Share a meal?

Z. Share a hug?

A. Share a life?

Z. Could we begin again?
   Rewind this spinnin earth?

A. Sell the planets?

Z. Blow away the clouds?

A. Vacuum up the sky?

Z. Stub out the sun?

A. Take the batteries out the birds and worms?

Z. Cillit Bang away the oceans?

A. Stuff the Big Bang back in its box?

Z. Are you happy?

A. Well. Loud noises still make me shake.

Z. When the girls hug me I tense up.

A. I'll never be able to eat in front of people.

Z. Sometimes I feel so lonely I just go to public toilets and cry.

A. I wee the bed. Soak the sheets right through.

Z. I'm scared my girls' love for me is goin to fade.
   Like they're goin to see me for who I really am.

A. I'm scared when I die
   this world won't pause.
   Cuz there'll be no family to remember me.
   I'll just fade away.

Z. Could we begin again?

A. Can I help you with somethin?

Z. Oh no I'm just lookin.

A. Well let me know if you need anythin.

   Have a great day.

The TWINS *look at each other and take a moment to take in what will never be.*

From the top?

Z. From the top.

A. Once upon a time we da Twins.

Z. We da Sharky Twins.
First name Baby.
Last name Sharky.

A. Winners of dat ultimate egg-and-spoon sperm race.
Waitin for our victory lap.

An explosion of sparkles and glitter pours down on them, coating them fully.
The TWINS *play and dance in the chaos.*

End of Play.

A Nick Hern Book

Wolfie first published in Great Britain in 2019 as a paperback original by Nick Hern Books Limited, The Glasshouse, 49a Goldhawk Road, London W12 8QP, in association with Theatre503, London

Wolfie copyright © 2019 Ross Willis

Ross Willis has asserted his moral right to be identified as the author of this work

Cover image by Rebecca Pitt

Designed and typeset by Nick Hern Books, London
Printed in Great Britain by Mimeo Ltd, Huntingdon, Cambridgeshire PE29 6XX

A CIP catalogue record for this book is available from the British Library

ISBN   978 1 84842 842 3

Woodland
CARBON
www.woodlandcarbon.co.uk
NICK HERN BOOKS
Printed on Carbon Captured paper